**Design Center
Stuttgart**

Focus Green

Internationaler
Designpreis
Baden-Württemberg
und
Mia Seeger Preis
2008

Baden-Württemberg
International
Design Award
and
Mia Seeger Prize
2008

avedition

Focus Green Inhalt

Focus Green Contents

4

**Internationaler
Designpreis
Baden-Württemberg
und
Mia Seeger Preis**

**Baden-Württemberg
International
Design Award
and
Mia Seeger Prize**

Ernst Pfister   MdL
Wirtschaftsminister
des Landes Baden-Württemberg

MP
Baden-Württemberg
Minister of Economic Affairs

»Was verbinden Sie mit der Farbe Grün?« Bei Grün denke ich an üppige Vegetation und assoziiere Leben sowie Wachstum mit dieser Farbe, ebenso Frische, Natürlichkeit und Hoffnung. Und hier sind wir bereits mitten im diesjährigen Thema des Designwettbewerbs 2008 – Focus Green widmet sich dem Umweltschutz und der Nachhaltigkeit beim Design.

Unsere Umwelt gilt es zu schützen gegen Menschen, die rücksichtslos mit ihr umgehen und diese zerstören, einseitig ausbeuten oder verschmutzen. Der Erhalt der Ressource Natur ist eine Aufgabe von jedem von uns. Wir alle sind moralisch verpflichtet, so zu leben, dass die Grundlage zukünftiger Generationen nicht gefährdet ist. Jedoch muss die Umsetzung von Nachhaltigkeitsstrategien wirtschafts- und sozialpolitisch verträglich erfolgen. Baden-Württemberg ist ein hochentwickelter Industriestandort. Energie und Rohstoffe sind wichtige Ressourcen mit entsprechend bedeutender Nachfrage. Allerdings verfügt Baden-Württemberg selbst über keine nennenswerten Rohstoff- und Energievorkommen, hat aber eine hohe Industriedichte und ist vergleichsweise dicht besiedelt. Diese Kombination führt dazu, dass ein besonderes Interesse am wirtschaftlichen und umweltschonenden Umgang mit natürlichen Ressourcen und Energien besteht.

Als Wirtschaftsminister setze ich mich für die Schaffung geeigneter Rahmenbedingungen ein. Bereits mit dem Umweltplan 2000 hat die Landesregierung Baden-Württemberg ihre Leitvorstellungen für eine dauerhaft umweltgerechte Entwicklung und für eine nachhaltige Zukunft des Landes vorgelegt. Dieser Umweltplan wird laufend fortgeschrieben. Darüber hinaus hat die Landesregierung Baden-Württemberg im April 2002 einen Nachhaltigkeitsbeirat berufen.

Nachhaltigkeit bedeutet, die wirtschaftlichen, sozialen und ökologischen Verhältnisse als eine Einheit zu betrachten. Leitziel für eine nachhaltige Entwicklung Baden-Württembergs ist demnach, die wirtschaftliche Leistungsfähigkeit des Landes, den sozialen Frieden, die natürlichen Lebensgrundlagen und die Lebensqualität der Bürgerinnen und Bürger zu erhalten. Dies bedingt, dass einerseits soziale und wirtschaftliche Entwicklungen zugleich umweltverträglich gesteuert werden und andererseits bei Umweltmaßnahmen auch deren soziale und wirtschaftliche Auswirkungen Berücksichtigung finden.

»What do you associate with the colour green?« When I think of green, I think of lush vegetation, and associate life and growth with this colour, as well as freshness, naturalness and hope. And this brings me right into the middle of this year's theme for the 2008 design competition – Focus Green is dedicated to design that takes its lead from environmental protection and sustainability.

Our environment has to be protected against people who treat it recklessly, destroy it, exploit it selfishly or pollute it. All of us are responsible for conserving the natural world as a resource. All of us have the moral duty to live in a way that does not jeopardize the living conditions of future generations. Nonetheless, sustainability strategies have to be pursued in an economically and socio-politically compatible way. Baden-Württemberg is an advanced industrial location. Energy and raw materials are important resources, and demand for them is correspondingly high. Baden-Württemberg itself does not have any appreciable sources of raw materials or energy, but it is highly industrialized and relatively densely populated. A combination like this means that there is a lot of interest in the economical and eco-friendly use of natural resources and energy.

As Minister of Economic Affairs and Technology, my job is to ensure that the right conditions are created. In its environment plan which it laid before the public as early as 2000, the Baden-Württemberg state government presented its blueprint for lasting, environmentally friendly development and for a sustainable future for the state. This environment plan is being continuously updated. In addition, the Baden-Württemberg state government appointed a sustainability council in April 2002.

Sustainability means considering economic, social and ecological exigencies as a unity. The overriding objective for the sustainable development of Baden-Württemberg, therefore, is to preserve the state's economic strength, social peace, the natural conditions needed for life, and the quality

Ökonomisches Handeln bedarf ökologischer Prinzipien, wenn es langfristig erfolgreich sein will. Umgekehrt kann in einer Industriegesellschaft nur derjenige auf Dauer ökologisch agieren, der die Gesetze der Ökonomie berücksichtigt. Daher ist es das Ziel der Landesregierung, allen Bürgern eine hohe Lebensqualität in einer ökologisch so gering wie möglich belasteten Natur zu ermöglichen.

Auf das Produktdesign übertragen bedeutet dies, dass wir Anreize zur Verlängerung der Lebensdauer und damit der Nutzungsdauer von Produkten geben wollen. Wiederverwertung und Recycling bestimmter Materialien zur Rückführung in den Material- und Wertstoffkreislauf werden immer wichtiger.

Bereits in der Koalitionsvereinbarung der Landesregierung ist das Ziel der Förderung innovativer Umwelttechnik festgehalten – hierin heißt es: »Innovative Umwelttechnologien sind Schlüsseltechnologien für die nachhaltige Entwicklung der Wirtschaftsstandorte. Wir werden deshalb Entwicklung und Verbreitung innovativer Umwelttechnik weiter fördern und insbesondere den Export umwelttechnischer Produkte aus Baden-Württemberg gezielt unterstützen.«

Die seit diesem Frühjahr vom Wirtschaftsministerium Baden-Württemberg bereitgestellten Innovationsgutscheine für kleine und mittlere Unternehmen können auch für Innovationen im Bereich der Nachhaltigkeit – speziell auch für Innovationen im Produktdesign – eingesetzt werden.

Den Nachhaltigkeitsaspekt gilt es auch beim Design konsequent umzusetzen. »Der Mensch ist nicht das Produkt seiner Umwelt – die Umwelt ist das Produkt des Menschen«, sagte schon Benjamin Disraeli (1804-81).

Der Internationale Designpreis Baden-Württemberg 2008, Focus Green, ist also auch ein Instrument, »grünen« Produktentwicklungen eine Plattform zu geben und damit die nach heutigen Standards besonders herausragenden Produktbeispiele einer breiten Öffentlichkeit zu präsentieren. Ich bin der festen Überzeugung, dass ökologische Produktentwicklung für die Unternehmen ein immer entscheidenderer Wettbewerbsfaktor wird. Schon jetzt ist Baden-Württemberg ein weltweit führendes Kompetenzzentrum für Umwelttechnik und Umweltforschung. Ich will diese Position weiter ausbauen und setze auf eine zielstrebige Forschungsförderung für modernste Umwelttechnik sowie den Export hochwertiger Produkte. In den globalen Märkten gewinnt die ökologisch orientierte Produktentwicklung aktuell an Bedeutung und zwar über alle

of life of all our citizens. On the one hand, this means that both social and economic developments have to be kept in tune with the environment and, on the other, that environment policies also have to be formulated with an eye to their social and economic effects. Economic action needs ecological principles if it is to be successful over the long term. Conversely, in an industrial society, actions can only be ecological in the long run if they consider the laws of economics. It is therefore the state government's objective to enable all its citizens to enjoy a high quality of life in an environment that is as untouched as possible.

When it comes to product design, this means that we want to provide incentives for making products' useful lives, and thus service lives, longer. Reusing and recycling certain materials, so that they are available as raw materials for new products, is becoming ever more important.

The objective of promoting innovative environmental technology is an integral part of the agreement establishing the state's coalition government. The agreement reads: »Innovative environmental technologies are key technologies for the sustainable development of industrial locations. We shall therefore continue to promote the development and dissemination of innovative environmental technologies and, above all, support the export of products made in Baden-Württemberg that feature environmental technology«.

The innovation vouchers for small and medium-sized enterprises that have been available from the Baden-Württemberg Ministry of Economic Affairs and Technology since the spring of this year can also be used for innovations in the area of sustainability, and especially also for innovations in product design.

Design also has to consistently give concrete form to the idea of sustainability. As Benjamin Disraeli (1804-81) might have said: »Man is not the creature of the environment, the environment is the creature of men«.

Focus Green, the Baden-Württemberg International Design Award, is therefore a way of giving »green« product developments a platform, and thus of presenting to a wide audience examples of products that we consider outstanding by our present-day standards. I am firmly convinced that ecological product development will become an ever more decisive competitive advantage for companies. Even now, Baden-Württemberg is a globally leading competence centre for environmental technology and research. It is my intention to build further on this lead. I believe

Branchen hinweg: von der Bauwirtschaft bis zu den Dienstleistern und selbst im Zusammenhang mit der Informationstechnologie; auf der diesjährigen CeBIT war zum Beispiel »green IT« ein herausragendes Thema.

Nachdem in früheren Jahren Unternehmen oft mehr ethisch motiviert umweltorientierte Produktpolitik betrieben, tun sie dies heute aus wirtschaftlicher Notwendigkeit. Auf Grund der explodierenden Energie- und Rohstoffpreise gibt es neue Anreize bei der Produktentwicklung wie zum Beispiel Materialreduzierung, minimale Konstruktionen oder Entwicklung von neuen Werkstoffen. Umweltorientiertes Wirtschaften und entsprechende Produkte werden für Unternehmen also mehr und mehr zur Selbstverständlichkeit. Trotzdem ist »grünes« Design immer noch ausbaufähig.

So hoffe ich, dass der diesjährige Designpreis Focus Green dazu beiträgt, dass in nachhaltigem Design Ökologie und Ökonomie weiter vereint werden können.

we can achieve this by supporting research into advanced environmental technology and by exporting high-quality products. In the global markets, ecologically driven product development is currently gaining in significance, whatever the industry. The spectrum ranges from construction to services, and even includes information technology: one of the prominent themes at this year's CeBIT trade fair was »green IT«.

Where companies once pursued eco-friendly product policy more for ethical reasons, nowadays they do so out of economic necessity. Soaring energy and raw materials prices give rise to new incentives in product development, such as reducing the quantities of materials used, reducing design to a minimum or developing new materials. Running businesses according to ecological criteria, and making products to match, is therefore becoming more and more the natural thing for companies to do. Even so, »green« design can still do more.

Accordingly, I hope that this year's Focus Green design award provides fertile ground for even greater harmonization of ecology and economy in sustainable design.

**Focus Green
2008**

Sabine Lenk   Leiterin des
                 Design Center Stuttgart

                 Head of
                 Design Center Stuttgart

Die erfolgreiche Teilnahme an Designwettbewerben bietet Unternehmen und Designstudios vielerlei Vorteile und stärkt die Position im Markt: Auszeichnungen sind ein Beleg für hohe Innovationskraft und positive Bestätigung der Leistungen in der Produktentwicklung. So avancieren die Preise zu einem Qualitätsmerkmal für Unternehmen und Produkte. Darüber hinaus stärken sie die Markenidentität, führen zu einer positiven Imagebildung und sind intern ein motivationssteigernder Faktor. Mit Designauszeichnungen bedachte Produkte leisten in der Regel einen wertvollen wirtschaftlichen und kulturellen Beitrag für Industrie und Gesellschaft.

Der Internationale Designpreis Baden-Württemberg, der als Staatspreis des Landes verliehen wird, hat ein unverwechselbares Profil. Die Auszeichnungen »Focus in Gold« und »Focus in Silber« sind begehrte Bestätigungen für höchste Designqualität. Jedes Jahr wird der Preis unter einem wechselnden Themenfokus ausgeschrieben, der sich an Belangen orientiert, die aktuell für Wirtschaft und Produktentwicklung maßgebend sind. Die Seriosität des Wettbewerbs und die nichtkommerzielle Ausrichtung wird durch die geringen Teilnahmegebühren gewährleistet, die es auch kleineren und mittleren Unternehmen ermöglichen, ihre Designleistungen im internationalen Umfeld zu testen. Besondere Fairness erfährt der Preis auch dadurch, dass die Jury bereits bei der Ausschreibung bekannt gegeben wird und deren eigene Produkte nicht am Wettbewerb teilnehmen können.

Thema 2008
Umweltschutz und Nachhaltigkeit sind Themen, die momentan die öffentliche und politische Diskussion bestimmen. Wie nie zuvor wird der Ruf – insbesondere auch in den internationalen Wachstumsmärkten und auf Leitmessen – nach umweltverträglichen Produkten immer lauter. Unternehmen und Designer haben darauf Antworten zu finden, die je nach Branche sehr unterschiedlich ausfallen können. Mal stehen Materialoptimierungen und Substitutionen im Vordergrund, dann wieder technisch orientiertere Maßnahmen zur Reduzierung des Energieverbrauchs während Herstellung und Gebrauch, und schließlich darf auch die formale Langlebigkeit nicht unterschätzt werden, die besonders entscheidend für die Nutzungsdauer und Umweltverträglichkeit eines Produktes ist. Agierten umweltbewusste Unternehmen in den 90er Jahren oft noch freiwillig als »Überzeugungstäter« und aus gesell-

Successful participation in design competitions offers companies and design studios a great many advantages, as well as strengthening their market position. Awards are evidence of outstanding innovative strength, and provide positive feedback on the work done in product development. In this way, awards also become quality criteria, for companies and products alike. In addition, they strengthen brand identity, lead to the formation of a positive image, and help to increase motivation internally. Award-winning products generally make a valuable economic and cultural contribution to business and society.

The Baden-Württemberg International Design Award, which is awarded as a government prize, has an unmistakable profile. The »Focus in Gold« and »Focus in Silver« design awards are highly sought after as guarantees of the highest design quality. Every year, contestants are invited to compete for this award with products focusing on a topic that changes from year to year, and that takes its lead from issues that are of decisive topical importance for the business world in general and product development in particular. Low participation fees guarantee the respectability and credibility of the competition, as well as its non-commercial nature, and also allow small and medium-sized enterprises to test their design work in an international environment. The award's fairness is also helped by the fact that the members of the judges panel are already known when the call for entries is made, and that their products may not take part in the competition.

The topic for 2008
Environmental protection and sustainability are topics that currently dominate public and political debate. As never before, the call for environmentally friendly products is becoming ever

schaftlicher Verantwortung, so bewirken heutzutage allein schon wirtschaftliche Zwänge eine Neuorientierung bei der Produktentwicklung. Denn ständig steigende Rohstoff- und Energiepreise verlangen Design, Engineering und Konstruktion intelligente Einsparungen ab.

Prämierung und Procedere

Am Internationalen Designpreis Baden-Württemberg nehmen Hersteller und professionelle Designer aus aller Welt mit Produkten in verschiedenen Kategorien teil. Die Markteinführung darf im längsten Fall zwei Jahre zurückliegen. Um Innovationen zu begünstigen, sind auch Prototypen zugelassen, deren Serienreife allerdings gewährleistet sein muss. Für Focus Green wurden 230 Produkte angemeldet, deren Hersteller und Designer unter anderem in Deutschland, Österreich, der Schweiz, Dänemark, den Niederlanden, Belgien, Großbritannien, Slowenien, Italien, den USA und Japan ansässig sind.

Die Produktprämierungen orientierten sich an den für Focus Green besonders wichtigen Geschäftsfeldern:
— Industrie und Gewerbe
— Architektur und Öffentlicher Raum
— Energie- und Gebäudetechnik
— Beleuchtung
— Medizin und Rehabilitation
— Bad und Sanitär
— Hausgeräte
— Küche
— Interior
— Objektmöblierung
— Kommunikation
— Freizeit und Outdoor
Bemerkenswert war es, dass es in der ursprünglich vorgesehenen Kategorie »Transport und Verkehr« nicht eine einzige Anmeldung gab.

Bei der Bewertung standen ökologische Designkriterien im Vordergrund. Dazu zählten:
— Potentielle Langlebigkeit durch formal zeitlose und qualitativ hochwertige Gestaltung
— Optionen für Servicemaßnahmen, Wartung und Reparatur
— Reduzierung des Rohstoffverbrauchs durch angepassten, minimierten Materialeinsatz
— Bevorzugte Auswahl von Materialien mit günstiger Umweltbilanz
— Art und Weise der Materialverwendung (als Einzelmaterial oder als Verbundmaterial beispielsweise)
— Berücksichtigung von sinnvollen und technisch machbaren Recyclingmöglichkeiten durch Materialkennzeichnungen und Konstruktionsprinzipien
— Herstellungsverfahren unter Berücksichtigung des Einsatzes von Hilfs- und Betriebsmitteln

louder, especially also in the international growth markets and at major trade fairs. It is up to companies and designers to find answers to these calls – answers that may differ greatly from industry to industry. Sometimes the focus is on optimized or substitute materials, sometimes on more technically oriented measures to reduce energy consumption during manufacture and use. Finally, formal longevity must not be underestimated, since it is especially decisive for how long a product is used, and thus for its environmental impact. While eco-conscious companies often acted voluntarily as »political activists« and out of a sense of social responsibility in the 1990s, economic constraints on their own are nowadays enough to bring about a new departure in product development. Constantly increasing raw materials and energy prices demand that design, engineering and construction deliver intelligent ways of economizing.

Awards and procedure

Manufacturers and professional designers from all over the world compete for the Baden-Württemberg International Design Award with products that fit into various categories. No more than two years must have passed since the products' market launch. To create a favourable environment for innovations, prototypes are also allowed to compete, provided their readiness for series production is guaranteed. A total of 230 products were entered for Focus Green. Their manufacturers and designers are based in countries such as Germany, Austria, Switzerland, Denmark, the Netherlands, Belgium, the UK, Slovenia, Italy, the U.S. and Japan.

For judging, the products were grouped into areas of business that are especially important for Focus Green:
— Industry and trade
— Architecture and public space
— Energy and installations technology
— Lighting
— Medicine and rehabilitation
— Bathrooms and sanitary installations
— Household appliances
— Kitchens
— Interiors
— Contract furniture
— Communication
— Leisure and outdoor activities
It was remarkable that there was not one entry in the »Traffic and transport« category, although such a category was planned.

Judging primarily focused on ecological design criteria. These included
— Potentially long service life thanks to formally timeless and high-quality design

— Energieverbrauch des Produkts bei a) Herstellung und b) im Gebrauch
— sowie begleitende Umwelterklärungen und Zertifikate zum Produkt

Aber auch die üblichen Kriterien zur Beurteilung guten Designs fanden Eingang:
— Gestaltungsqualität
— Innovationsgehalt
— Ergonomie
— Verwendung neuer Werkstoffe
— Gebrauchsqualität
— Benutzerführung, Produktgrafik bzw. Typographie
— Wertigkeit, Anmutung, emotionaler Gehalt
— Gestalterische Qualität der Produktausstattung: Bedienungs-, Montageanleitung, Verkaufsverpackung

Zwei Tage lang prüften die Experten der Jury die eingereichten Produkte, die im Original in Augenschein genommen wurden. Für die möglichst objektive Bewertung ist die Beurteilung am Original ein Muss, und es gibt zuvor keine bereits selektierende Fotojury.

Ergebnisse
Die außergewöhnlich hohe Qualität der Einreichungen führte zu einem Rekordergebnis bei »Focus in Gold«: Elfmal wurde die Premiumauszeichnung vergeben, die gemäß des Reglements maximal einem Produkt pro Kategorie zugesprochen wird. 55 weitere Produkte zeichnete die Jury mit einem »Focus in Silber« aus. Alle 66 Preisträger sind auf den folgenden Seiten ausführlich mit Jurykommentaren veröffentlicht. Außerdem stellen wir Ihnen die Jurymitglieder und deren persönliches Statement zu umweltorientierter Produktgestaltung vor. Ein weiterer Teil der Publikation zeigt die Preisträger und Anerkennungen des Mia Seeger Preises für Junior-Designer.

Schließlich profitieren alle erfolgreichen Unternehmen und Gestalter von einer mehrwöchigen Ausstellung im Werkzentrum Weststadt in Ludwigsburg, die bis zum 30. November 2008 läuft, sowie von der Präsentation im Internet.

— Options for servicing, maintenance and repair
— Reduced use of raw materials thanks to appropriate, minimized use of materials
— Preference given to materials with a favourable eco-balance
— Way in which materials are used (as non-composite or composite materials, for example)
— Consideration of sensible and feasible possibilities for recycling, either by labelling materials or in the design principles used
— Manufacturing processes that consider the use of auxiliary and consumable materials
— Energy consumption of the product during a) manufacturing and b) use, and
— Any environmental declarations and certificates accompanying the products

But consideration was also given to conventional criteria for assessing good design:
— Design quality
— Innovative content
— Ergonomics
— Use of new materials
— Quality of use
— User controls, product graphics and typography
— Quality, grace, emotional content
— Design quality of product peripherals: instructions for use and assembly, sales packaging

For two days, the experts on the judges panel assessed the submitted products, which they were able to inspect in the original. Assessing the original product is a must to allow judging to be as objective as possible. There is no judging on the basis of photographs to pre-select products.

Results
The outstandingly high quality of the products submitted led to a record result in the »Focus in Gold« class. This ultimate accolade was awarded eleven times. The competition rules only allow one product per category to receive this award. The judges awarded the »Focus in Silver« to a further 55 products. All 66 award-winners are published in detail on the pages that follow, together with the judges' comments. We also present the members of the panel and their own personal views on eco-friendly product design. In a further part of this publication, we present the prize-winning and highly commended entries for the Mia Seeger Prize for young designers.

Finally, all the award-winners will enjoy the additional benefit of having their products exhibited at Werkzentrum Weststadt in Ludwigsburg until 30 November 2008, as well as being presented in the internet.

Erfolgsrezept –
attraktiv und vermarktbar:
Ästhetik mit ökologischen Inhalten.
Industrie beschäftigt sich
verstärkt mit Nachhaltigkeit.

Recipe for success –
attractive and marketable:
aesthetics with ecological content.
Industry is increasingly con-
cerning itself with sustainability.

**Focus Green
2008**

Roland Heiler   Geschäftsführer des Porsche Design Studio
in Zell am See, Österreich

General Manager of the Porsche Design Studio
in Zell am See, Austria

Nach seiner Ausbildung zum Technischen Zeichner bei Porsche in Zuffenhausen studierte Roland Heiler Design am Royal College of Art in London. Im Anschluss begann er als Designer im Exterieur-Studio bei Porsche zu arbeiten. Später wurde er Leiter des Konzept-Studios und anschließend Leiter des Bereiches Design Services bei Porsche. Für drei Jahre führte ihn 1997 sein beruflicher Weg als Leiter für Exterieur Design zu Audi nach Ingolstadt. Im Jahr 2000 wurde er Chefdesigner im Porsche Styling-Studio in Huntington Beach, Kalifornien; zwei Jahre später übernahm er dessen Leitung. Seit 2004 ist er Geschäftsführer des Porsche Design-Studios in Zell am See.

After training as a draughtsman at Porsche in Zuffenhausen, Roland Heiler studied design at the Royal College of Art in London, before returning to Porsche to work as a designer in the exterior-equipment studio. Later he was appointed head of the concept studio, and then head of Design Services at Porsche. In 1997 he moved to Audi in Ingolstadt for three years, where he was head of exterior-equipment design. In 2000, he became chief designer in the Porsche Styling Studio in Huntington Beach, California, and assumed overall responsibility for the studio two years later. Since 2004, he has been general manager of the Porsche Design Studio in Zell am See.

Die Verbraucher haben das Bedürfnis, Produkte zu kaufen, die unsere Umwelt nicht schädigen, also keine negativen Auswirkungen während der Herstellung und bei der Entsorgung haben. Wichtig ist, diese ökologischen Produkte so zu gestalten, dass sie zudem attraktiv und vermarktbar sind.

Im Wettbewerb konnten wir verschiedene Aspekte beobachten. Zum einen werden ganz neue Materialien entwickelt, die dort eingesetzt werden, wo reine Naturprodukte Nachteile haben. Beispielsweise ist ein Terrassenbelag aus einem Kompositmaterial, das aus Recycling-Kunststoff und Holz besteht, ökologisch sinnvoller als ein reiner Holzbelag. Zum anderen werden wieder vermehrt Geräte produziert, die mit Handkraft betätigt werden, wie eine Küchenwaage, ein Rührgerät oder ein Rasenmäher.

Auch das ökologische Bewusstsein der Hersteller ist heute sehr ausgeprägt. Sowohl die Fachleute im Bereich Design, aber auch in der Konstruktion und Produktion, beschäftigen sich verstärkt mit dem Thema »Nachhaltigkeit«.

Gutes Design zeichnet sich dabei immer durch den Einklang von Ästhetik und Funktion aus – und das ist auch die Philosophie unseres Hauses. Produkte, die nur ökologisch aber nicht ästhetisch inspiriert sind, können sich nicht durchsetzen. Deshalb halte ich es für ein Erfolgsrezept, Ästhetik mit ökologischen Inhalten zu verbinden. Wir haben im Wettbewerb Beispiele gesehen, die schon ein sehr hohes Niveau hatten, aber es gibt noch eine Menge zu tun.

Consumers feel the need to buy products that do not harm our environment: in other words, products that create no negative impact during their manufacture and their disposal. It is important to design these ecological products so that they are also attractive and marketable.

In this competition, we could see various aspects. On the one hand, completely new materials are being developed and used where purely natural products are at a disadvantage. For example, patio tiling made of a composite material manufactured from recycled plastic and wood makes more ecological sense than using wood alone. On the other hand, more and more appliances are being produced that are operated manually, such as a kitchen scales, a whisk or a lawnmower.

Today's manufacturers also have a heightened ecological awareness. Experts in the areas of design, construction and production are devoting more and more attention to the »sustainability« issue.

Good design always results from the harmony of aesthetics and function – and this is also our studio's philosophy. Products that are simply ecological without being inspired do not have a chance. That's why I believe the recipe for success is to combine aesthetics with ecological content. In this competition, we have seen examples that have already achieved a very high standard, but there is still a lot to do.

Focus Green
2008

Nicola Stattmann   Produktdesignerin, Büro Nicola Stattmann
Material_Technologie_Produktentwicklung, Frankfurt

Product designer, Büro Nicola Stattmann
Material_Technologie_Produktentwicklung, Frankfurt

Materialforschung –
Bio-Kunststoffe statt petrochemische
Werkstoffe. Niedrigkomplexe Materialien
modifiziert bis zu Solar-Zellen-Papier.

Materials research –
bio-plastics instead of petrochemical
materials. Modified low-complex materials,
all the way to solar-cell paper.

Nicola Stattmann ist eine international anerkannte Expertin im Bereich Materialien und Design. Sie studierte Produktdesign an der Hochschule der Bildenden Künste Saar in Saarbrücken. Nach ihrem Studium war sie nicht nur wissenschaftlich tätig, sondern arbeitete in dem Designbüro von Uwe Fischer in Frankfurt und später als Manager Material Research bei designafairs in München. Seit 2002 ist Nicola Stattmann selbstständig und spezialisiert auf neue Materialien, Technologien und Produktentwicklung. Leitkriterium in den daraus resultierenden Projekten ist insbesondere Ökologie. Zahlreiche Veröffentlichungen und Gastprofessuren sowie die Kooperation mit Hochschulen und Forschungseinrichtungen.

Nicola Stattmann is an internationally recognized expert in the area of materials and design. She studied product design at the Saar Academy of Fine Arts in Saarbrücken. After graduating, she continued to work academically, as well as working in Uwe Fischer's design studio in Frankfurt and later as manager for materials research at designafairs in Munich. Nicola Stattmann has worked freelance since 2002, specializing in new materials, technologies and product development. Her guiding criterion in the projects resulting from this specialization is ecology. She has written many publications and held many visiting professorships, and has cooperated with universities and research institutes.

Der Wettbewerb zeigt, dass es inzwischen viele Massenprodukte gibt, die auf schlaue Weise ökologisch sind. Eine wachsende Nachfrage ist der Grund dafür. Zu den »Welt-Retter-Kunden« sind die anspruchsvollen »Gesundheits-Kunden« hinzugekommen. Ein wachsendes Bewusstsein für ökologische Zusammenhänge wird unsere Produktwelt enorm verändern.

Für die Produktentwicklung sollte es zukünftig selbstverständlich sein, dass ökologische Kriterien von Anfang an in den Entwicklungsprozess integriert werden. Nur durch die Berücksichtigung von Konstruktions- und Produktionskriterien wie zum Beispiel Leichtbau, Monomaterial, Volumen- und Komponentenreduzierung, Einsparung von Prozessschritten, energiearme Herstellungsverfahren, Miniaturisierung etc. sowie die Nutzung von ressourcenschonenden Rohstoffen können glaubhaft ökologische Produkte entstehen.

In den 1980er Jahren, als »Jute statt Plastik« aufkam, begann die Forschung mit der Entwicklung von ökologischen Werkstoffen. Die Entwicklung von Kunststoffen aus nachwachsenden Rohstoffen begann mit Plastiktüten-Kunststoffen und ist heute bei high-tech Kunststoffen angekommen. Diese Bio-Kunststoffe verfügen über extrem gute mechanische Eigenschaften und können in vielen Produktbereichen petrochemische Werkstoffe ersetzen.

Außerdem beschäftigt sich die Forschung damit, preiswerte und niedrigkomplexe Materialien durch bestimmte Zusatzstoffe, Beschichtungen oder Modifikationen mit anspruchsvollen Eigenschaften auszustatten. So wird zum Beispiel Papier wetterfest, feuerfest, zu Keramik, formgeschäumt, extrudiert... und bald soll es sogar »Solar-Zellen-Papier« geben.

Wenn solche Materialien dann schlau eingesetzt werden, dann sind wir auf einem guten Weg.

This competition shows that there are now many mass products that are cleverly ecological. The reason is growing demand. »Save the world customers« have now been joined by demanding »health customers«. Growing awareness of ecological issues will profoundly change our product world.

In the future, it should be a matter of course for product development that ecological criteria are an integral part of the development process, right from the start. Only if consideration is given to design and production criteria such as lightweight construction, monomaterial, reduction of volume and components, fewer process stages, low-energy manufacturing processes, miniaturization, etc., as well as to the use of raw materials that conserve resources, will it be possible to create credibly ecological products.

When the »jute instead of plastic« movement started in Germany in the 1980s, researchers began developing ecological materials. The development of plastics from renewable resources began with plastic bags, and has now arrived in the domain of high-tech plastics. These bio-plastics have extremely good mechanical properties, and can replace petrochemical materials in many product areas.

In addition, researchers are looking at ways of giving inexpensive, low-complex materials sophisticated properties, by adding certain ingredients, coatings or modifications. For example, paper will be weatherproof, fireproof, a ceramic, foamed, extruded – and soon they say there will even be »solar-cell paper«.

If materials like these are then applied cleverly, we will be on the right path.

Focus Green
2008

Designstudenten – sensibilisieren für:
Ökologie; Produkte mit Lebenszyklus und Wiederverwertung; Substitution
von Wegwerfprodukten.

Create a feeling in design students for:
ecology, products with a life cycle and recycling,
substitution of disposable products.

Alex Terzariol   Industriedesigner
MM Design GmbH, Brixen

Industrial designer
MM Design GmbH, Brixen (Bressanone)

Nach seinem Studienabschluss am Istituto Europeo di Design in Mailand war Alex Terzariol als Senior Designer bei Bonetto Design in Mailand zunächst für die Automobilindustrie im Centro Stile Fiat Auto tätig. 1991 gründete er das Studio MM Design in Brixen, das sich ausschließlich mit Industriedesign für verschiedene Branchen befasst. Zahlreiche dort entwickelte Produkte wurden mit internationalen Designpreisen ausgezeichnet. Gemeinsam mit anderen industrienahen Dienstleistern der Region Bozen hat MM Design das Projekt »Metamorphosis« initiiert – eine Kooperation zu Ecodesign, Nachhaltigkeit und Lebenszyklus-Konzepten. Alex Terzariol lehrt außerdem als Dozent an verschiedenen italienischen Universitäten, unter anderem in Venedig / Treviso.

After graduating from the Istituto Europeo di Design in Milan, Alex Terzariol worked as senior designer for Bonetto Design in Milan, initially for the automotive industry in the Centro Stile Fiat Auto. In 1991 he founded the MM Design studio in Brixen, which focuses solely on industrial design for various sectors. Many of the products developed there have won international design awards. Together with other industry-linked service providers in the Bozen (Bolzano) region, MM Design has initiated the »Metamorphosis« project – an alliance for ecological design, sustainability and life cycle concepts. Alex Terzariol also lectures at various Italian universities, including Venice-Treviso.

Als Designer bin ich überzeugt davon, dass wir alle eine neue Sensibilität gegenüber dem Thema »Nachhaltigkeit und Umwelt« entwickeln müssen. Als Dozent möchte ich meine Studenten für ökologisches Design sensibilisieren und vor allem drei wichtige Themen vermitteln.

Erstens um eine Sensibilisierung und ein Bewusstsein für Ökologie zu erreichen, muss man Produkten ein gutes Design geben, damit man eine enge und vor allem emotionale Beziehung mit ihnen eingeht. Sie leben mit mir, sie altern mit mir, wie wenn es Leder oder Holz wäre. Mit der Zeit fühle ich mich mit ihnen emotional verbunden, das heißt, sie sind zu etwas geworden, das zu mir gehört, und damit zu nachhaltigen und langlebigen Produkten.

Zweitens das Thema Wiederverwertung: Es muss ein kritisches Bewusstsein entwickelt werden, damit Produkte nicht nur zur Montage, sondern auch zur einfachen Demontage immer im Zusammenhang mit ihrem Lebenszyklus entworfen werden. Wenn das gelingt, ist es möglich, Produkte zu realisieren, die, wenn sie nicht mehr gebraucht werden, wiederverwertet werden können: ihre Materialien, teilweise ihre Komponenten oder sogar das ganze Produkt.

Das dritte Thema ist Substitution. Bei uns in Italien kommen zum Beispiel einmal im Jahr neue Telefonbücher. Jedes Mal muss man Unmengen von Bäumen dafür abholzen. Heute ist es möglich, das Telefonbuch per Internet abzurufen. Das bedeutet eine wesentlich geringere Umweltbelastung. Wenn also die Entwerfer fähig sind, Dinge, die sowieso weggeworfen werden, durch andere, die die Umwelt weniger belasten, zu ersetzen, sind wir auf dem richtigen Weg.

Wir alle müssen uns darum kümmern, was wir unseren Kindern hinterlassen. Wir müssen versuchen, mit unserer Arbeit dazu beizutragen, die Probleme zu lösen, aber sie dürfen nicht mehr werden.

As a designer, I am convinced we all have to develop a new sensitivity for »sustainability and environment«. As a lecturer, I want to create a feeling for ecological design in my students, and above all to communicate three important topics.

First, in order to achieve sensitivity for and consciousness of ecology, products must be given a good design, so that people develop a close, and above all emotional, relationship to them. They live with me, grow old with me, as though they were leather or wood. As time goes by, I develop emotional ties to them. In other words, they have become something that belongs to me, and have thus become sustainable and long-living products.

Second, the topic of recycling. A critical awareness has to be developed, so that products are not only designed to be assembled, but also to be disassembled, always in connection with their life cycle. It this is successful, it will be possible to make products that can be recycled when they are no longer needed: their materials, sometimes their components, or even the entire product.

The third topic is substitution. In Italy, for example, new telephone directories are published once a year. Countless trees have to be felled for this. Today, it is possible to access the telephone directory by internet. This means far less environmental impact. So if designers are capable of replacing things – things that will be thrown away anyway – by others that have less impact on the environment, we will be on the right path.

All of us have to care about what we leave behind for our children. In our work, we have to try to help solve problems. What we mustn't do is create more problems.

Ursula Tischner   Jury
Judges panel

**Focus Green
2008**

Ursula Tischner   Industrie-Designerin
econcept, Agentur für nachhaltiges Design, Köln
Associated Professor an der Design Academy Eindhoven, Niederlande

Industrial designer
econcept, Agentur für nachhaltiges Design, Cologne
Associated Professor at the Design Academy Eindhoven, Netherlands

Subtile Ökologie –
attraktive Produkte, die Ökologie
und bessere Produktqualitäten integrieren
und das auf emotionale Art erzählen.

Subtle ecology –
attractive products that integrate
ecological and enhanced product qualities,
and convey this emotionally.

Ursula Tischner arbeitete vier Jahre am Wuppertal Institut für Klima, Umwelt und Energie. 1996 gründete sie in Köln econcept und berät seitdem Unternehmen, führt Forschungsprojekte durch und gestaltet Produkte und Dienstleistungen. Das Ziel ist dabei immer die ökonomische, ökologische und soziale Nachhaltigkeit von Produktions- und Konsumsystemen zu vergrößern. Außerdem ist sie als Expertin für Sustainable Design in verschiedenen Netzwerken, Juries und Gremien, wie zum Beispiel ISO oder DIN, tätig. Gemeinsam mit ihr hat das Design Center Stuttgart bereits erfolgreiche Projekte umgesetzt, zum Beispiel 2000 den internationalen Design-Kongress »Towards sustainable development« und 2005 die Veranstaltung »ecobiente«. Sie ist Autorin zahlreicher Fachbücher zu Design und Ökologie. Seit 2002 lehrt sie an der Design Academy Eindhoven.

Ursula Tischner worked for four years at the Wuppertal Institute for Climate, Environment and Energy. In 1996, she founded econcept in Cologne. Since then, she has advised companies, managed research projects, and designed products and services. In all these activities, her goal is to improve the economic, ecological and social sustainability of production and consumer systems. She also works as an expert for sustainable design in various networks, juries and committees, such as ISO or DIN. The Design Center Stuttgart has already carried out successful projects with her, such as »Towards Sustainable Development«, the international design conference in 2000, and »ecobiente« in 2005. She has written many textbooks on design and ecology. She has been a professor at the Design Academy Eindhoven since 2002.

Designer und Unternehmen sollten mit viel größerem Selbstbewusstsein ökologische Produkte auf den Markt bringen. Es gibt Produkte, die einen modernen Ökologiebegriff vertreten, wie das Sofa von Brühl – ein schönes trendiges Sofa. Schaut man genau hin, merkt man, dass Bezüge austauschbar sind und ökologische Materialien verwendet wurden. Wir nennen das subtile Ökologie.

Und genau das brauchen wir: attraktive Produkte, die gleichzeitig Ökologie integrieren, bessere Produktqualitäten zeigen und das so erzählen, dass der Konsument es versteht, also nicht hochwissenschaftlich, sondern auf emotionale Art. Dann mögen die Leute das auch.

Man kann von einem Produkt nicht erwarten, dass es alle ökologischen Designkriterien erfüllt. Es gibt kurz- und langlebige, hoch- und niedrigpreisige Produkte, die unterschiedlich gestaltet sein müssen. Aber für alle gibt es immer eine ökologischere Gestaltungsstrategie. Die müssen Designer suchen und so umsetzen, dass es stimmig ist, sowohl was den Preis als auch die Ästhetik und die ökologischen Aspekte angeht. Man kann sich im einen Fall auf das Recycling konzentrieren und im anderen auf die Materialauswahl.

Designer haben oft noch Vorurteile gegenüber Ökologie und ein Halbwissen, wie: Plastik und Aluminium sind schlecht. Die Informationen müssen leichter verfügbar sein und für Designer besser aufbereitet werden. Es muss bessere Ausbildungsmöglichkeiten geben. Die Designer sollten sich selbst einen Wissenspool, eine Art Datenbank, aufbauen, mit Projekten anfangen, dazulernen und Materialkompetenz entwickeln. Dann sind wir auf dem richtigen Weg.

Designers and companies should be much more self-assured when marketing ecological products. There are products that stand for a modern notion of ecology, like the Brühl sofa – an attractive, trendy sofa. On closer inspection, you notice that the covers can be replaced, and that ecological materials have been used. We call this subtle ecology.

And that's exactly what we need: attractive products that integrate ecology, manifest enhanced product qualities, and convey this in a way consumers can understand – not in an over-intellectual way, but emotionally. Then people will love the products, too.

You cannot expect a product to fulfil every criterion of ecological design. There are short- and long-lived, high- and low-price products, and all of them have to be designed differently. But for all of them, there is always a more ecological design strategy. Designers have to find and pursue this strategy so that the product makes sense: in terms of price, aesthetics and ecology. In one instance, the focus may be on recycling. In the next, on the choice of materials.

When it comes to ecology, designers often have preconceived notions and superficial knowledge. For example, they say that plastic and aluminium are bad. Information has to be more easily accessible, and processed better for designers. There have to be better opportunities for training. Designers should establish their own pool of knowledge, a kind of database. They should get started on projects, learn new things and develop knowledge of materials. Then we will be on the right path.

20

**Focus Green
2008**

Andrew Wong   Produktdesigner
Frog Design, Herrenberg

Product designer
Frog Design, Herrenberg

Zukunftsvision –
kein »Öko-Design« mehr, weil es selbstverständlich ist. Defizite noch in der Politik, bei
Herstellern und Konsumenten.

My vision of the future –
no more ecological design, because it is
taken for granted. Politicians, manufacturers and
consumers still have some catching up to do.

Nach seinem Produktdesign-Studium an der Swinburne School of Design in Australien, das er mit dem BA abschloss, machte Andrew Wong seinen Diplomdesigner an der Fachhochschule Hildesheim/Holzminden/Göttingen. Heute ist er Senior Designer bei Frog Design in Herrenberg. In den letzten sechs Jahren arbeitete er an Designlösungen mit zahlreichen Kunden, wie beispielsweise Motorola, Disney, Unilever, BSkyB, SIT Group, Liebherr, UPC, Maggi und Teuco. Seine Projekterfahrungen reichen von Medizin, CE, Industrie bis zu Privatkunden, Möbeln und Verpackung.

After graduating from the Swinburne School of Design in Australia with a B.A. in product design, Andrew Wong studied for a design diploma at the Hildesheim, Holzminden and Göttingen University of Applied Sciences. Today, he is senior designer at Frog Design in Herrenberg. Over the past six years, he has worked on design solutions for many clients including Motorola, Disney, Unilever, BSkyB, SIT Group, Liebherr, UPC, Maggi and Teuco. His project experience ranges from medicine, CE and industry to private clients, furniture and packaging.

Bei der Nutzung von ökologisch sinnvollen Produkten muss man heute keine Kompromisse mehr machen. Weder im Design, noch in der Funktionalität oder im Image. Ein gutes Beispiel für kompromisslose Gestaltung und Umweltverträglichkeit ist der Tesla Roadster, ein elektrisch angetriebenes Auto aus den USA, das locker mit einem Ferrari oder Porsche mithalten kann.

Ein gutes ökologisches Produkt muss einfach ein gutes Produkt sein. Es soll vor allem kein Unterschied zu herkömmlichen Produkten erkennbar sein. Im Gegenteil: Es muss gut oder besser funktionieren, es muss gut oder besser aussehen und es muss im Gebrauch auf jeden Fall günstiger oder energiesparender sein. Und es darf auf keinen Fall mehr kosten.

Die Frage, um die sich alles dreht, ist, wer die Initiative zu einem Umdenken anstößt. Denn es gibt noch einige Defizite in der Politik, bei Herstellern und Konsumenten. Wenn die Konsumenten die Nutzung von ökologischen Produkten ausdrücklich bevorzugen, werden sie eine Politik unterstützen, die entsprechende Gesetzesinitiativen erlässt. Dann würde die Herstellung zum Beispiel umweltfreundlicher Handys unterstützt werden. Liegt die Initiative bei den Unternehmen, dann wird sich nur jenes umweltfreundliche Produkt am Markt etablieren, welches sich rechnet. Erste Ansätze auf beiden Seiten sind bereits da. Ich bin optimistisch, dass sich dieser Prozess fortsetzt.

Als Designer können wir helfen, die beste Strategie zu finden und zu zeigen: es ist möglich, dass ein Produkt schön aussehen, gut funktionieren und umweltverträglich sein kann. Meine Hoffnung ist, dass es in der Zukunft kein »Öko-Design« mehr gibt und man nicht mehr über nachhaltiges Design spricht, weil es für alle selbstverständlich ist. Hoffentlich schon in den nächsten zehn Jahren.

Today, there is no longer any need for compromises when it comes to using products that make ecological sense. Neither when it comes to design, nor to function, nor to image. One good example of uncompromising design and environmental compatibility is the Tesla Roadster, an electrically driven car from the U.S. that can easily hold its own against a Ferrari or Porsche.

A good ecological product simply has to be a good product. Above all, it should not differ noticeably from conventional products. On the contrary: it must function well, if not better, it must look good, if not better, and it must certainly be more inexpensive, or more energy-saving, to use. And on no account must it cost more.

The key question is: who will provide the initiative for a rethink? As I see it, politicians, manufacturers and consumers still have some catching up to do. If consumers explicitly opt to use ecological products, they will support politicians who propose draft legislation in this direction. Then support would be given, for example, to the manufacture of environmentally friendly mobile phones. If it is up to companies to provide the initiative, then the only environmentally friendly products that become established on the market will be those that make a profit. There are already the first signs of movement on both sides. I am optimistic that this process will continue.

As designers, we can help to find and point out the best strategy: it is possible for a product to look good, function well and be environmentally compatible. My hope for the future is that there will no longer be any ecological design, and people will no longer speak about sustainable design, but everyone will take it for granted. Let's hope it happens in the next ten years.

**Focus Green
2008**

Martin Zentner   Grafikdesigner, Stuttgart

Graphic designer, Stuttgart

Ökologisches Design –
spart Geld und hat somit Zukunft.
Weg von der Abgrenzungspolitik der Hersteller
durch unterschiedliche Normen.

Ecological design –
saves money, and so it has a future.
Manufacturers should abandon their isolationist
policies of differing standards.

Martin Zentner studierte zunächst Informatik in Tübingen, bevor er auf die Freie Kunstschule in Stuttgart in das Fach Grafikdesign wechselte. Nach seinem Abschluss im Jahr 2000 war er dort als Dozent für Editorial Design tätig und stieg als Art Director in die Zeitschrift Design Report ein. 2002 übernahm er die Chefredaktion des Magazins und leitete es bis Ende des Jahres 2007. 2008 wurde er Art Director der Konradin Mediengruppe und war verantwortlich für das Corporate Design des Verlages mit über 45 Zeitschriften. Im Juli 2008 machte er sich mit einem Grafikbüro selbstständig.

Before switching to graphic design at the Freie Kunstschule art academy in Stuttgart, Martin Zentner studied computer science in Tübingen. After graduating in 2000, he became a lecturer in editorial design at the academy, and joined the magazine »Design Report« as art director. In 2002, he became the magazine's editor-in-chief, and remained in this position until the end of 2007. In 2008, he became the art director of the Konradin media group, where he was responsible for the corporate design of the publishing house's more than 45 magazines. In July 2008 he became a freelancer, with his own graphics studio.

Ökologisches Handeln ist in der Regel auch ökonomisch. Ein Produkt, das wenig Rohstoffe verbraucht, ist nicht nur besser für die Umwelt, sondern auch besser für den Geldbeutel. Wenn es Geld spart, dann ist jeder gerne umweltbewusst. Meine Zukunftsvision: Rohstoffe werden immer teurer. Produkte, die verschwenderisch damit umgehen, werden aus wirtschaftlichen Gründen verschwinden. Ökologisches Design spart Geld und hat somit Zukunft.

Das oberste Kriterium für gutes ökologisches Design bedeutet für mich die Frage: braucht man dieses Produkt überhaupt? Hat es eine Funktion, und sei es auch lediglich eine emotionale? Manche Produkte haben zwar keine direkte Funktion, aber sie machen uns glücklich. Es gibt jedoch Produkte, mit denen keiner glücklich wird. Sie sollen Bedürfnisse stillen, die von Marketingexperten erst geweckt wurden.

Für mich ist es zudem unökologisch, dass es keine einheitliche Norm für Speicherkarten, Akkus und Ladegeräte gibt. Kauft man eine neue Kamera oder ein neues Mobiltelefon, kann man das alte Zubehör in der Regel wegwerfen. Da hilft es auch nicht, wenn das Zubehör aus nachhaltigen Materialien gefertigt ist. Großes ökologisches Potenzial sehe ich im Abschied der Hersteller von ihrer Abgrenzungspolitik durch unterschiedliche Normen. Dadurch würde sich die Zahl der Produkte verringern. Weniger Müll und geringere Produktionskosten wären das wünschenswerte Ergebnis.

As a rule, to act ecologically is also to act economically. A product that consumes less raw material is not only better for the environment, but also saves money. And if money can be saved, then everyone is willing to be environmentally conscious. My vision of the future: raw materials will become more and more expensive. Products that use these resources wastefully will disappear, for economic reasons. Ecological design saves money, and so it has a future.

For me, the acid test of good ecological design is: do we really need this product? Does it serve any function, even if only an emotional one? Some products do not serve any direct function, but they make us happy. But there are products nobody can be happy with. They are designed to satisfy needs that were artificially aroused by admen.

I also think it is unecological that there are no universal standards for memory cards, rechargeable batteries and battery chargers. If you buy a new camera or mobile phone, you can generally throw away all your old accessories. Then it no longer matters if those accessories are made of renewable materials. There is huge ecological potential to be tapped if manufacturers abandon their isolationist policies of differing standards. This would reduce the number of products. Less rubbish and lower production costs would be the – welcome – result.

Focus in Gold

Sonic TC™ Akustische Materialprüfanlage
Acoustic materials testing unit

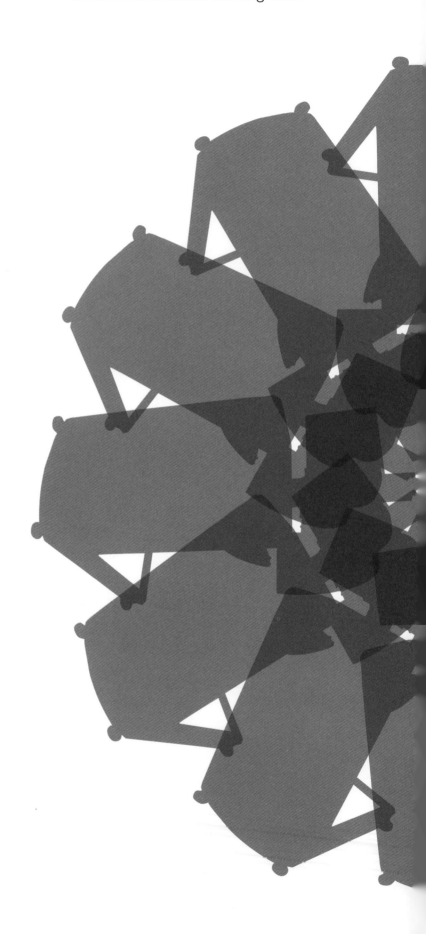

26

**Industrie und Gewerbe
Gold**

**Industry and trade
Gold**

Sonic TC™   **Akustische Materialprüfanlage
Acoustic materials testing unit**

Hersteller / Manufacturer
RTE Akustik + Prüftechnik GmbH
D-76327 Pfinztal/Karlsruhe

Design / Designer
bgp-design
Knut Braake, Stefan Grobe
D-70563 Stuttgart

Vertrieb / Distributor
RTE Akustik + Prüftechnik GmbH
D-76327 Pfinztal/Karlsruhe

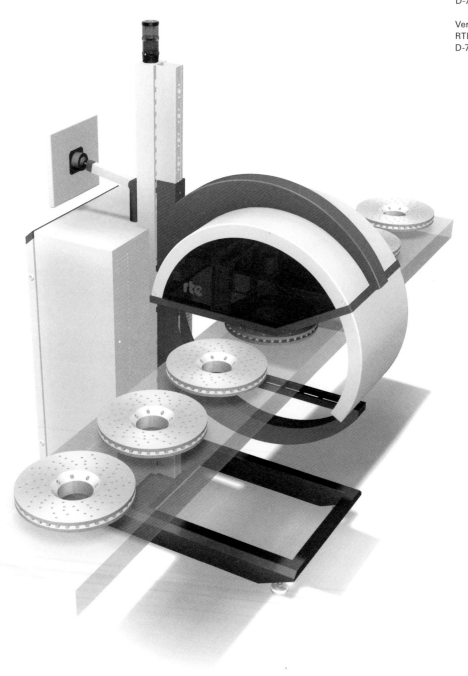

Jury
Durch den Einsatz von Schall bei der
Materialprüfung werden hochenergie-
verbrauchende Techniken, wie Rönt-
gen, oder der Einsatz von Chemikalien
vermieden. Mit dem Einsatz einer neuen
Technologie werden Ressourcen geschont. Gut ist, dass direkt im Produktionsprozess geprüft werden kann und
Ausschuss sofort festgestellt wird. Dann
kann die Produktion entsprechend verändert werden.

Judges panel
The use of sound waves for materials testing means that extremely energy-intensive X-ray technology can be avoided, as
well as the use of chemicals. The use of
a new technology conserves resources.
It is good that testing can be done directly in the production process, and re-
jects can be spotted immediately. Production can then be modified accordingly.

Die Anlage »Sonic TC™« arbeitet mit einer völlig
neuen und revolutionären Prüftechnik. Wo früher
zeit- und energieaufwändige Prozesse notwen-
dig waren, reicht hier ein kurzer mechanischer Im-
puls aus. Und sie arbeitet zerstörungsfrei und
ressourcenschonend ohne Einsatz von Chemikalien oder energieintensiver Röntgentechnologie.

Bremsscheiben, Gussteile oder auch keramische
Produkte werden während des Durchlaufs auf
dem Band in Schwingung versetzt. Ein Hochleis-
tungsmikrofon erfasst ihren Klang, den ein Prüf-
rechner vollautomatisch auswertet und mit Refe-
renzparametern vergleicht. Innerhalb nur einer
Sekunde liegt ein detailliertes Ergebnis über die
Qualität des Prüfobjekts vor.

Pro Stunde können bis zu 4500 Prüfteile – on the
fly, also im schnellen Durchlauf – direkt auf einem Transportband auf Gefügefehler, Risse oder
Lunker geprüft werden.

Im weiteren Verlauf kann die Steuerung einen
Auswerfer oder eine Markiereinheit ansteuern,
um die fehlerhaften Teile kenntlich zu machen.
Die kompakte und autarke Funktionseinheit ist
eine reine Stahlblechkonstruktion, die entsprechend dem rauen Produktionsumfeld sehr wider-
standsfähig und langlebig ist. Dank der flexibel
gestalteten Struktur kann »Sonic TC™« an unterschiedlichste Transportbänder angebracht
werden ohne zusätzlichen mechanischen und
elektrischen Aufwand. So lässt sich die Anlage
in verschiedenen Produktionsprozessen flexibel
einsetzen – ein wirtschaftlicher Vorteil.

The »Sonic TC™« unit uses a completely new, revolutionary testing technology. Where time and
energy-intensive processes were once necessary, it makes do with a brief mechanical pulse.
Moreover, it works non-destructively and in a
resource-conserving way, without the need for
chemicals or energy-intensive X-ray technology.

As they pass along the belt, brake disks, cast parts
or even ceramic products are vibrated. A high-
performance microphone records the sound they
make, and a testing computer automatically evalu-
ates this sound and compares it with reference
parameters. Within just once second, the system
delivers a detailed analysis of the quality of the
test object.

Every hour, up to 4,500 parts can be tested on
the fly directly on the conveyor belt – for struc-
tural faults, cracks or sink holes.

As the parts move on, the control unit can command that the parts are thrown out or marked
as defective.

This compact, self-contained unit is made exclusively of sheet steel, which gives it the toughness
and durability it needs in a rough production environment. Thanks to its flexibly designed structure,
»Sonic TC™« can be attached to a wide variety
of conveyor belts with no need for any additional
mechanical or electrical adjustment. This means
that the unit can be used flexibly in different production processes, which in turn saves money.

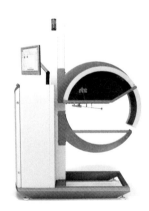

FG 5002/5005E   Plasmagenerator
Plasma generator

Industrie und Gewerbe
Silber

Industry and trade
Silver

FG 5002/5005E   **Plasmagenerator**
Plasma generator

Hersteller / Manufacturer
Plasmatreat GmbH
D-33803 Steinhagen

Design / Designer
bgp-design
Knut Braake, Stefan Grobe
D-70563 Stuttgart

Vertrieb / Distributor
Plasmatreat GmbH
D-33803 Steinhagen

Jury
Sehr gut, dass Nasschemikalien zur
Reinigung von Alubändern nicht mehr
verwendet werden müssen und dadurch keine Entsorgungsprobleme entstehen. Die innovative Technologie
macht die Vorbereitungsprozesse in der
Produktion effizienter, lösungsmittel-
und chemikalienfrei. Und trägt so zur
ökologischen Effizienz des Produktions-
prozesses bei.

Judges panel
Very good to see that liquid chemicals
no longer have to be used to clean aluminium sheets, so that there are no more
disposal problems. This innovative technology makes preparatory processes in
production more efficient, with no need
for solvents or other chemicals. In this
way, it helps make the production process
ecologically efficient.

Der Hochspannungsgenerator erzeugt atmo-
sphärisches Plasma (Open Air®). Dieses ist ein
neu entwickeltes, wirtschaftliches und umwelt-
verträgliches Verfahren zur Reinigung, Aktivie-
rung und Beschichtung von Oberflächen aus
Kunststoff und Metall, beispielsweise bei Falt-
schachtelveredelungen, Spritzgusstechnik,
Beschichtung von CDs, Anwendungen in Mikro-
elektronik, Medizin- und Textiltechnik oder im
Automobil-, Schiff- und Flugzeugbau. Dem viel-
seitigen Einsatz der atmosphärischen Plasmabe-
handlung sind kaum Grenzen gesetzt.

Gerade bei der Verarbeitung von Aluminium sind
die häufigsten Probleme der korrosive Angriff
von Oberflächen, Restkontaminationen von Walz-
ölen und die heute angewandten umweltbeein-
trächtigenden und energiereichen Vorbehand-
lungsverfahren.

Diese Probleme können dank dieser innovativen
Technologie auf ein Minimum reduziert oder sogar
völlig eliminiert werden. So kann bei der atmosphärischen Plasmatechnologie Open Air® bei
Reinigungs- und Vorbehandlungsprozessen
unter anderem auf den Einsatz von umweltbelas-
tenden Lösungsmitteln verzichtet werden.

Der Plasmagenerator ist modular aufgebaut und
so gestaltet, dass er hervorragend zugänglich ist.
Ein übersichtliches Klartext-Display gibt Informationen zum Generator, den Plasmadüsen und
zum Service. Das klare, präzise Design spiegelt
die innovative Prozesstechnologie nach außen
wider.

This high-voltage generator produces atmospheric plasma (Open Air®). Plasma is used in a
newly developed, economical and environmentally friendly process for cleaning, activating and
coating plastic and metal surfaces. It is used to
treat folding cartons, in injection moulding and
when coating CDs, and its applications range from
micro-electronics, medical and textiles technology, to automotive engineering, shipbuilding and
aircraft construction. There is hardly any limit to
the many uses of atmospheric plasma treatment.

Especially when processing aluminium, the most
frequent problems are surface corrosion, residual contamination of rolling oils and the currently
used pre-treatment processes, which are both pol-
luting and energy-intensive.

Thanks to this innovative technology, these problems can be reduced to a minimum, or even ruled
out altogether. When cleaning and pre-treating
using Open Air® atmospheric plasma technology,
for example, there is no need for harmful solvents.

The plasma generator is modular in construction,
and designed so that it can be accessed easily.
An easy-to-read clear-text display provides information about the generator and the plasma noz-
zles, as well as about when servicing is due. The
innovative process technology is reflected in
the generator's clear, precise design.

ERMB Drehmodul
Rotary module

Industrie und Gewerbe
Silber

Industry and trade
Silver

ERMB **Drehmodul**
Rotary module

Hersteller / Manufacturer
Festo AG & Co. KG
D-73734 Esslingen

Design / Designer
Werksdesign / In-house design
Karoline Schmidt

Vertrieb / Distributor
Festo AG & Co. KG
D-73734 Esslingen

Jury
Das Ökologische an dem Produkt ist,
dass es aus Aluminium ist, das man recyceln kann. Aber vor allem überzeugt,
dass es sich um ein Modul handelt, das
in unterschiedlichste Maschinen eingebaut werden kann. Sehr guter ökologischer Ansatz. Bemerkenswert: dank
einer besonderen Konstruktion braucht
man keinerlei zusätzliche Schmierstoffe.
Extrem langlebig. Hat eine funktionale
puristische Schönheit.

Judges panel
What is ecological about this product is
the fact that it is made of aluminium,
which can be recycled. But what is especially impressive is that it is a module
that can be installed in the widest variety
of machines. Very good ecological ap-
proach. One remarkable feature is the
special design that obviates the need
for any additional lubricants. Extremely
long-lasting. Functional, purist elegance.

Dieses Drehmodul lässt sich mit einer Vielzahl
geeigneter Motoren kombinieren und damit für
jeden Einsatzbereich anpassen. Der elektrische
Drehantrieb mit Zahnriemen sticht durch einen
unbegrenzten Drehwinkel hervor. Der Antrieb
verfügt an allen Seiten über Befestigungsmög-
lichkeiten und lässt sich in jeder Lage einbauen.
So kann er zum Beispiel als Frontend an einem
bestehenden Achssystem oder eigenständig
als Drehtisch eingesetzt werden. Er wird in drei
Baugrößen und mit verschiedenem Zubehör
angeboten.

Dank Kugellager ist es möglich, das Drehmodul
ohne zusätzliche Schmierstoffe einzusetzen.
Eine robuste Antriebswelle im Innern bietet eine
hohe Lebensdauer. Das Modul lässt sich komplett zerlegen. Der hohe Metallanteil, vor allem
Aluminium und Stahl, führt zu hohen Recycling-
quoten. 95 Prozent der Teile können wiederverwertet werden.

Das Design ist technisch, klar und präzise und
betont die kompakte Bauform des Drehantriebs.
Der Drehbereich um die zentrale Achse wird
hervorgehoben und verdeutlicht so die Funktionsweise.

This rotary module can be combined with a large
number of suitable motors, and thus adapted
for every area of use. Equipped with a toothed belt,
this electrical rotary drive can be turned to any
angle. With mounting options on all sides, the drive
can be installed in any position. For example, it
can be used as a front end for an existing axis system, or on its own as a turntable. It is available in
three sizes, and with a range of accessories.

Thanks to its ball bearings, the rotary module can
be used without any additional lubricant. A sturdy
motor shaft gives it a long service life. The module can be completely broken down, and the high
proportion of metal used, especially aluminium
and steel, means that it can almost completely be
recycled. Ninety-five percent of the parts can be
recycled.

The design is technical, clear and precise, and emphasizes the compact construction of the rotary
drive. The turning area around the central axis is
accentuated, highlighting the way the drive works.

TSC 1   Auflagenleisten-Reiniger
Slat cleaner

Industrie und Gewerbe
Silber

Industry and trade
Silver

TSC 1   **Auflagenleisten-Reiniger**
Slat cleaner

Hersteller / Manufacturer
Trumpf Grüsch AG
Elektrowerkzeuge
CH-7214 Grüsch GR

Design / Designer
IKTD
Institut für Konstruktionstechnik und Technisches Design
Universität Stuttgart
Thomas Maier
D-70569 Stuttgart

Vertrieb / Distributor
Trumpf Werkzeugmaschinen GmbH & Co. KG
D-71254 Ditzingen

Jury
Der Vorteil des Gerätes ist, dass man Auflagenleisten bei Laserschneidanlagen
mehrmals reinigen kann, bevor sie ausgetauscht werden müssen. Damit entsteht weniger Abfall. Und es wird Zeit ge-
spart. Ergonomisch gut durchdacht.
Fantastisch, dass sogar kleine Frauen mit
diesem Gerät arbeiten können.

Judges panel
The advantage of this tool is that the
support slats of laser cutting machines
can be cleaned several times before
they have to be replaced. This means
there is less waste. And time is saved,
too. Ergonomically well thought through.
It's fantastic that even short women
can work with this tool.

Der »TSC 1« ist ein neuartiges Elektrowerkzeug,
mit dem man Auflagenleisten fast aller gängigen
Flachbettlasermaschinen schnell und sicher reinigen kann; denn sind Laserschneidanlagen ver-
schmutzt, wird nicht nur der Prozess unsiche-
rer, auch die Qualität der gefertigten Teile sinkt.

Bisher wurden verschmutzte Auflageleisten
entweder sofort erneuert oder manuell mit Ham-
merschlägen und selbstgebauten Werkzeugen
in mehreren Stunden harter Arbeit gereinigt. Dank
der Reinigung mit dem neuen Elektrowerkzeug
können die Auflagenleisten mehrfach verwendet
werden, was Rohstoffe, Ressourcen und Geld
spart.

Das Gerät funktioniert folgendermaßen: Zwei
Walzenpaare zertrümmern die Schlacke, die sich
auf den Leisten befindet. Dank seines automatischen Vorschubs ist die Bedienung einfach und
mühelos, der Mitarbeiter muss hauptsächlich
die Maschine über die Querleisten führen. Das Gerät ist ergonomisch so gestaltet, dass auch eine
kleine Bedienperson im aufrechten Stand und mit
ausgestrecktem Arm den Griff erreichen kann.

The »TSC-1« is an innovative power tool that can
be used to clean the support slats of almost any
conventional flatbed laser machine quickly and re-
liably. If laser cutting machines are dirty, the process not only becomes less stable, but the quality
of the finished parts also suffers.

Up to now, dirty support slats either had to be
immediately replaced or cleaned manually – a process that involved a lot of hard work with ham-
mers and tools constructed in-house. Cleaning
with this new power tool means that slats can
be used several times, and this saves raw materials, resources and money.

The appliance works as follows: two pairs of rol-
lers crush the slag that has formed on the slats.
Thanks to its automatic forward feed, operation
is simple and effortless – the operator's main
task it to guide the machine over the slats. The
appliance is ergonomic in design, which means
that even short operators can reach the handles
standing up and with outstretched arms.

ICE Ketten
Chains

Industrie und Gewerbe
Silber

Industry and trade
Silver

ICE   Ketten
         Chains

Hersteller / Manufacturer
RUD Ketten Rieger & Dietz GmbH & Co. KG
D-73432 Aalen–Unterkochen

Design / Designer
Werksdesign / In-house design

Jury

Durch eine Materialinnovation, also hochfesten Stahleinsatz, wird die Materialmenge reduziert. So braucht es weniger Material im Vergleich zu Vorgängermodellen, was natürlich grundsätzlich sehr ökologisch ist. Das geringere Gewicht bedeutet aber auch Reduzierung von Energie und Kraftstoff etc. beim Transport. Bemerkenswert das Materialkodierungssystem: bei zu extremen Temperaturen verändert sich die Farbe. Dann muss das Produkt ausgewechselt werden, weil es verschlissen ist.

Judges panel

An innovation in the material used – high-tensile steel – reduces the amount of material needed for this product. Because it uses less material than its predecessor models, it is fundamentally very ecological. However, its reduced weight also means that less energy and fuel is needed for transport. The material coding system is remarkable: if temperatures exceed a certain limit, the colour changes. Then the product has to be replaced, because it is worn out.

Die Kette ist um bis zu 60 Prozent fester und 30 Prozent härter als Vorgängermodelle, aber auch um über 30 Prozent leichter und wesentlich unempfindlicher gegenüber Verschleiß. Eingesetzt wird sie beispielsweise bei Tieftemperaturen bis minus 60°C in Alaska, Sibirien, Polargebieten oder auf Bohrinseln.

Bei dieser Kette ist es erstmalig gelungen, eine durchgehende Nenndickenreduzierung auch für Ketten mit kleineren Durchmessern als 16 Millimeter gegenüber Güteklasse 8 zu erreichen. Das ist dank der enormen Festigkeit eines neuartigen, patentierten Stahles, einer speziellen Formgebung und spezifischer Verarbeitung möglich. Damit ist eine völlig neue Klasse – Güteklasse 12 – erreicht.

Dank dieser innovativen Entwicklung wird der Rohstoff- und Ressourcenverbrauch deutlich reduziert und gleichzeitig die Qualitäts- und Leistungsmerkmale verbessert. Die spezielle ICE-Pink-Pulverbeschichtung signalisiert dauerhaft die Temperatur, in welcher die ICE-Kette maximal eingesetzt wurde. Beim verbotenen Einsatz über 300°C wird aus pink braunschwarz. Das zeigt an, dass die Kette ausgetauscht oder zur Instandsetzung zum Hersteller gebracht werden muss.

The chain is up to 60 percent tougher and 30 percent harder than predecessor models, but also more than 30 percent lighter and far less susceptible to wear. It is used, for example, in low temperatures of up to minus 60°C in Alaska, Siberia and polar regions, or on oil rigs.

This chain is the first time a consistent reduction in nominal thickness compared with quality class 8 has been achieved, also for chain links with material diameters of less than 16 millimetres. This is possible thanks to the extreme toughness of a novel, patented steel, to a special design, and to special finishing. As a result, a new quality class – class 12 – is achieved.

Thanks to this innovative development, the use of raw materials and resources is significantly reduced, while quality and performance are improved. The special ICE pink powder coating permanently displays the maximum temperature at which the ICE chain was used. When it is used above the maximum permitted temperature of 300°C, the pink turns brown-black. This means that the chain has to be replaced or returned to the manufacturer for repair.

Industrie und Gewerbe   Industry and trade
Silber   Silver

Design Tech   **Mehr-Etagen-Laminator**
              Multi-layer lamination system

Hersteller / Manufacturer
Robert Bürkle GmbH
D-72250 Freudenstadt

Design / Designer
Design Tech
Jürgen R. Schmid
D-72119 Ammerbuch

Vertrieb / Distributor
Robert Bürkle GmbH
D-72250 Freudenstadt

Jury
Die Produktsprache verrät, dass es bei
der Maschine um Solarpaneele geht. Das
sonnige Gelb erinnert sofort an die Sonne und die kristalline Struktur der Paneele,
die die Maschine verkleiden, symboli-
siert die Solarpaneele, die dort laminiert
werden. Für ein Investitionsgüterde-
sign ist es fast schon emotional und im
Zusammenhang mit dem zu laminie-
renden Produkt sehr schlüssig gestaltet.

Judges panel
The product language betrays the fact
that this machine has to do with solar
panels. The sunny yellow is an immediate
reminder of the sun, and the crystalline
structure of the panels encasing the
machine symbolizes the solar panels that
are laminated there. As capital goods
go, this design is almost emotional. Its
design makes sense in connection with
the product to be laminated.

Photovoltaikmodule sind empfindliche Bauteile.
Ihre Oberflächen müssen durch eine Laminie-
rung vor Beschädigungen geschützt werden. Das
erreicht diese Anlage, auf der synchron auf mehreren Etagen Photovoltaikmodule laminiert werden
können.

Die vier Funktionselemente – Beladung, Laminier-
presse, Kühlpresse und Entladung – sind hinter
einer selbsttragenden kulissenähnlichen Verkleidung untergebracht. Diese nimmt in ihrer Produktsprache durch die Kassettierung das Motiv
der Solarmodule auf.

Die Funktionselemente – Be- und Entladung –
werden besonders hervorgehoben, indem sie als
eigene Volumen ausgebildet sind. Zwischen
Verkleidung und Anlage befinden sich Wartungs-
räume, die schnell zugänglich sind. Durch ein
außen angebrachtes Bedienpaneel kann der Pro-
zessablauf direkt kontrolliert werden.

Photovoltaic modules are sensitive components.
Their surfaces have to be laminated to protect
them against damage. This is what this system
does, simultaneously laminating photovoltaic
modules in several layers.

The four functional elements – loading, encapsu-
lation, cooling and unloading – are located behind a self-supporting panel that is reminiscent of
a backdrop in the theatre. In its product language,
with sunken panels, this backdrop alludes to the
solar module theme.

The functional elements – loading and unloading – are given special emphasis by giving them
their own formally discrete spaces. Maintenance
space, which can be accessed quickly, is provided
between the panel and the system. An operating panel attached on the outside of the unit allows the process to be controlled directly.

HDS 10/20-4 M Hochdruckreiniger
High-pressure cleaner

Industrie und Gewerbe
Silber

Industry and trade
Silver

HDS 10/20-4 M **Hochdruckreiniger**
High-pressure cleaner

Hersteller / Manufacturer
Alfred Kärcher GmbH & Co. KG
D-71364 Winnenden

Design / Designer
Werksdesign / In-house design
Denis Dammköhler
und
Pearl Creative
Tim Storti und Christian Rummel
D-71636 Ludwigsburg

Vertrieb / Distributor
Alfred Kärcher Vertriebs-GmbH
D-71364 Winnenden

Jury
Dieses Gerät ist ökologisch, weil man Temperatur, Energieverbrauch und Reinigungsmittel dosieren kann, je nach Grad der Verschmutzung. Das macht Sinn. Es ist ein Zusatzfeature zu einem normalen Hochdruckreiniger, das einen ökologischen Umgang mit dem Gerät ermöglicht. Schön auch die Interface-Gestaltung mit der Eco-Einstellung, damit die Leute vielleicht doch motiviert werden, in der effizienten Stufe zu reinigen.

Judges panel
This appliance is ecological because temperature, energy consumption and detergent can be determined exactly, depending on how much dirt has to be moved. That makes sense. It is an additional feature to a normal high-pressure cleaner that allows the appliance to be used ecologically. The way the interface has been designed, with the eco setting, is also well done, and could well motivate people to clean using this efficient setting.

Der Heißwasser-Hochdruckreiniger »HDS 10/20-4 M« verbindet effektivste Reinigungskraft und Mobilität mit Umweltschutz, Betriebssicherheit sowie Bediener- und Servicefreundlichkeit.

Um energieeffizient zu arbeiten, lässt sich die Wassertemperatur von 20 bis 155°C variieren. Viele Verschmutzungen können jedoch schon bei Temperaturen von rund 60°C leicht entfernt werden. Dafür lässt sich am Hauptschalter die sogenannte Eco-Stufe fest einstellen und damit der Kraftstoffverbrauch um bis zu 20 Prozent reduzieren. Die Reinigungsmittel können von 0,5 bis 6 Prozent präzise dosiert werden. Das erhöht nicht nur die Wirtschaftlichkeit, sondern ist auch umweltschonender.

Umweltaspekte werden im gesamten Produktionsprozess wie zum Beispiel lösungsmittelfreie Pulverbeschichtung oder Wasserrecycling beim Funktionstest berücksichtigt. Der Hochdruckreiniger ist recyclinggerecht konstruiert und lässt sich, wenn er manuell zerlegt wird, um bis zu 95 Prozent recyceln. Um die Aufbereitung zu erleichtern, wurden alle Kunststoffteile mit ihrer Materialart gekennzeichnet.

Außerdem ist der Hochdruckreiniger sehr langlebig, Ersatzteile werden viele Jahre zur Verfügung gestellt. Auch das macht ihn zu einem umwelt- und ressourcenschonenden Produkt.

The »HDS 10/20-4 M« hot-water high-pressure cleaner combines the most effective cleaning power and mobility with environmental protection, operating safety and ease of service.

To allow work to be done energy-efficiently, the water temperature can be varied between 20 and 155°C. However, many stains can easily be removed even at temperatures of around 60°C. This is the temperature of the eco setting, which can be selected permanently at the main switch, and reduces fuel consumption by as much as 20 percent. The cleaning agents can be measured out precisely in dosages of between 0.5 and 6 percent. This not only makes it more economical to use, but also reduces its environmental impact.

Environmental aspects are considered throughout the entire production process, such as solvent-free powder coating or water recycling during the function test. The high-pressure cleaner is designed to satisfy recycling considerations. When it is broken down manually, it is up to 95 percent recyclable. To make recycling easier, all the plastic parts have been marked to show what they are made of.

In addition, the high-pressure cleaner is very long-lasting, with spare parts available for many years. This, too, makes it a product that helps protect the environment and conserve resources.

40

Industrie und Gewerbe
Silber

Industry and trade
Silver

PW 6101   **Gewerbliche Waschmaschine**
Commercial washing machine

Hersteller / Manufacturer
Miele & Cie. KG
D-33332 Gütersloh

Design / Designer
Werksdesign / In-house design
Andreas Enslin

Vertrieb / Distributor
Miele & Cie. KG
D-33332 Gütersloh

Jury
Viele Technologien zum Sparen von Energie, Wasser und Waschmittel werden eingesetzt, wie Wasserrückgewinnung oder dass Restwärme für den nächsten Waschprozess gespeichert und die benötigte Heizenergie dadurch gesenkt werden kann. Da die Waschmaschine sehr groß ist, muss man sich nicht mehr bücken, sie ist also auch für etwas ältere Benutzer gut geeignet. Die wunderschöne Waschtrommel mit Wabenstruktur ist ein gutes Beispiel für Bionik. Gut und ansprechend gestaltetes Produkt.

Judges panel
Many technologies have been used to save energy, water and detergent, such as water recovery or the storage of residual heat for the next wash cycle, which reduces the amount of heating needed. As the washing machine is very big, there is no need to bend down to load or unload it – this makes it suitable for slightly older people as well. Its elegant, honeycomb-structured drum is a good example of bionics. Good, attractively designed product.

Die Gewerbemaschine zeichnet sich durch ihre herausragende Nachhaltigkeit aus. Sie lässt sich mit einer Wasserrückgewinnung ausstatten. Das bedeutet bis zu 30 Prozent Wassereinsparung. Darüber hinaus kann auch Restwärme für den nächsten Waschgang gespeichert werden. Beimischungen im letzten Spülbad, wie zum Beispiel Imprägnierungen, werden gezielt aufgefangen und lassen sich dadurch wiederverwenden.

Ein integriertes Wiegesystem dosiert je nach Wäschemenge nicht nur den Wasser- und Waschmittelverbrauch, sondern auch die Energiemenge.

Optimal geschont wird die Wäsche dank der patentierten Schontrommel. Durch die wabenförmige Oberflächenstruktur entsteht ein Wasserfilm, auf dem die Wäsche sanft gleitet. Das sehr große Trommelvolumen reduziert die Waschvorgänge pro Tag.

Die Gewerbemaschine besticht auch durch ihre sehr elegante, klare Gestaltung.

This commercial washing machine stands out by virtue of its excellent ecological features. It can be equipped with a water recovery system. This means a water saving of up to 30 percent. In addition, residual heat can be stored for the next wash cycle. Additives to the final rinse cycle, such as impregnating agents, are deliberately captured, and can be used again.

An integrated weighing system meters not only the water and detergent needed for the volume of washing, but also the energy needed.

The laundry is given the gentlest possible treatment thanks to the patented garment-protecting drum. Its honeycomb surface structure creates a film of water on which washing can gently glide. The very large volume of the drum means that the number of wash cycles per day is reduced.

This commercial machine is also striking in design – it is very elegant and uncluttered.

Nannette Hopf   Bügelhandmaß
Ironing gauge

Industrie und Gewerbe
Silber

Industry and trade
Silver

Nannette Hopf   **Bügelhandmaß**
Ironing gauge

Hersteller / Manufacturer
Ätztechnik Herz GmbH & Co.
D-78736 Epfendorf

Design / Designer
Nannette Hopf
D-70839 Gerlingen

Vertrieb / Distributor
Nannette Hopf
D-70839 Gerlingen

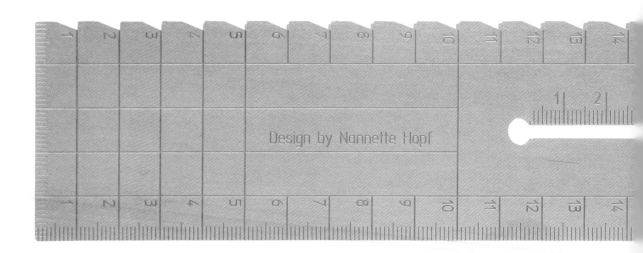

Jury
Ökologisch sehr sinnvolles Produkt. Die Handmaße aus Kunststoff schmelzen beim Bügeln und müssen anschließend weggeworfen werden. Dieses hier ist aus Edelstahl und kann auch noch an nächste Generationen vererbt werden. Schön gemacht und gut gestaltet.

Judges panel
This product makes a lot of sense ecologically. Plastic gauges melt when ironed, and then have to be thrown away. This one is made of stainless steel, and can be handed down from one generation to the next. Beautifully made, and well designed.

Das Hand- und Bügelmaß wird in Schneidereien verwendet. Es dient als Anzeichenhilfe für Knopflöcher, Nahtzugaben, Falten, Radien und ganze Kreise. Außerdem lassen sich damit Ecken und Säume ausbügeln, ohne dass Nadeln benutzt werden müssen. Mehrere beidseitig präzise geätzte Skalen und Linien erleichtern das Messen von kleinen Abständen und ermöglichen ein Arbeiten ohne Abstecken durch Nadeln.

Im Gegensatz zu herkömmlichen Handmaßen, die aus Kunststoff sind und Bügelhitze und heißem Wasserdampf nicht standhalten, ist das neue patentierte Bügelhandmaß aus Edelstahl. Damit ist es hitze- und dampfresistent und kann problemlos als Bügelhilfe eingesetzt werden. Die sehr hochwertige Verarbeitung mit gratfreien und stumpfen Kanten macht das Werkzeug zu einem Augen- und Handschmeichler.

Das langlebige, nachhaltige Produkt ist recycelbar und wird in einem süddeutschen umweltzertifizierten Betrieb gefertigt, in dem auch das Lasern und Ätzen erfolgt. Das spart Transportwege und weitere Emissionen.

This gauge is used by tailors. It is used to help mark buttonholes, seam allowances, pleats, radii and whole circles. It also allows corners and hems to be ironed without any need for pins. Precisely calibrated scales and lines on both sides make it easier to measure small distances, and allow work to be done without pinning.

Unlike conventional gauges, which are made of plastic and cannot withstand heat from irons or hot steam, this new, patented gauge is made of stainless steel. This makes it resistant to heat and steam, and means it can be used without difficulty as an ironing aid. Its high-quality finish, with deburred, bevelled edges makes the tool visually attractive and pleasant to hold.

This long-lasting product is recyclable, and manufactured in an environmentally certified factory in south Germany, which also performs the lasermarking and etching work. This keeps transport to a minimum, and reduces emissions.

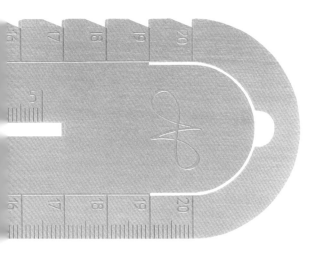

Focus in Gold   GrüneWand® Begrünte Innenraumwände
Planted interior walls

GrüneWand® Begrünte Innenraumwände
Planted interior walls

**Architektur und Öffentlicher Raum
Gold**

**Architecture and public space
Gold**

GrüneWand® **Begrünte Innenraumwände
Planted interior walls**

Hersteller / Manufacturer
H+W Bewässerungs GmbH
D-84364 Birnbach

Design / Designer
Indoorlandscaping GmbH
D-54295 Trier

Vertrieb / Distributor
Art Aqua GmbH & Co.
D-74321 Bietigheim-Bissingen

Jury

Diese grüne Wand ist besonders reiz-
voll, weil man den Garten in die Vertikale
bringt und auch in Gebäuden großflächig Grünpflanzen anbieten kann. Ein ökologisches und außerdem sehr ästhe-
tisches, charmantes Produkt. Es ist nicht
nur sinnvoll für die physische Gesundheit, sondern spielt auch eine psycholo-
gische Rolle. Es steigert das Wohlbefin-
den, reinigt die Luft, reduziert Schadstoffe
und erhöht die Konzentrationsfähigkeit.

Judges panel

This green wall is especially appealing
because the garden has been transposed
to the vertical plane, and allows large
surfaces of green plants to be displayed
inside buildings as well. An ecological
as well as extremely aesthetic and charming product. Not only does it make
sense health-wise, but it also plays a psy-
chological role. It enhances the sense
of well-being, cleans the air, reduces toxic
fumes and promotes concentration.

Die »GrüneWand®«, eine eingetragene Produkt-
lösung, regelt auf natürliche Weise das Raum-
klima, neutralisiert Schadstoffe, wie sie beispielsweise bei Luftbefeuchtern auftreten, bindet Staub
und spart Energie.

In der Regel wurzeln die Pflanzen bei Begrünungs-
projekten im Boden und wachsen senkrecht
nach oben. Hier dagegen werden die Pflanzen in
eine vertikal stehende Wand gepflanzt. Die Klima-
anlage aus der Natur gibt es in zwei Varianten: eine
mobile und eine fest montierte Version.

Bei den beweglichen Wänden, die als visuelle
und akustische Raumteiler eingesetzt und beidseitig begrünt werden können, ist das Wasser-
reservoir in einem Edelstahlbehälter unter der grünen Wand untergebracht. Bei der festen Wand
wird der Behälter entweder wie bei der mobilen
Variante oder aber in einem Technikraum unter-
halb der Wand verstaut, wodurch Wartungen unauffälliger durchgeführt werden können.

Der Aufbau einer grünen Wand besteht aus einer
Edelstahl-Unterkonstruktion und den stabilen
Vegetationsplatten, die in einer Gärtnerei etwa
14 bis 18 Wochen mit Bodendeckern vorkultiviert
werden. Über eine Zeitsteuerung werden Be-
wässerung, Verdunstung und damit in gewissem
Umfang auch die Raumluftfeuchtigkeit geregelt.
Wird die grüne Wand nicht mehr gebraucht, kann
sie einfach kompostiert werden.

»GrüneWand®« (literally »green wall«), a patented
product solution, controls the indoor climate
naturally, neutralizes noxious fumes (which hu-
midifiers produce, for example), traps dust and
saves energy.

In schemes to make rooms greener, plants are
generally rooted at floor level and grow vertically
upwards. In this solution, however, the plants
are set in a vertical wall. This natural air-condition-
ing system is available in two versions: one mobile, the other fixed.

In the movable walls, which can be used as visual
and acoustic room partitions, and which can be
planted on both sides, the water tank is located in
a stainless-steel container under the green wall.
In the fixed wall, the tank is either stored away in
the same way as in the mobile partition or in a
utility room elsewhere in the building, which allows maintenance work to be carried out with
less inconvenience.

A »GrüneWand®« comprises a stainless-steel
substructure and the robust vegetation panels,
which are preplanted with ground-covering vegetation in a nursery 14 to 18 weeks before deliv-
ery. A time switch controls irrigation and evapor-
ation, and thus also room humidity to a certain
extent. If the green wall is no longer needed, it can
simply be composted.

Plusenergiehaus® Modulbau
Modular building

**Architektur und Öffentlicher Raum
Silber**

**Architecture and public space
Silver**

Plusenergiehaus® **Modulbau
Modular building**

Hersteller / Manufacturer
Rolf Disch
SolarArchitektur
D-79100 Freiburg

Design / Designer
Werksdesign / In-house design

Vertrieb / Distributor
Rolf Disch
SolarArchitektur
D-79100 Freiburg

Jury
Ein Fertighaus, das modular aufgebaut ist und man in verschiedenen Größen und Anordnungen haben kann. Und das Beste an diesem Gebäude ist, dass es ein Plusenergiehaus® ist, das mehr Energie produziert als die Bewohner verbrauchen und sogar noch Strom ins Netz liefern kann.

Judges panel
A prefabricated house that is modular in structure and available in various sizes and configurations. The best thing about this building is that it is a Plusenergiehaus® that generates more power than its occupants consume, and can even feed electricity into the grid.

Das Plusenergiehaus® erzeugt mehr Energie als verbraucht wird. Mit der Weiterentwicklung zu einem modularen System lässt das Holzhaus aus wohngesunden Baustoffen sich noch vielseitiger verwenden: als Einzel-, Doppel- oder Reihenhaus. Man kann flexibel reagieren auf jede spezifische Nutzung, Raumbedarf, Grundstückssituation, Bebauungspläne – durch optionalen Anbau, variable Geschossigkeit, alternative Dachformen, verschiedenste Raumaufteilungen, sogar mit Aufzug und barrierefrei.

Der Bauprozess ist dank der variantenreichen Bausteine und einer vorgefertigten Powerbox sehr viel effizienter. Diese Powerbox ist die energetische Schaltzentrale für Strom und Wärme, Wasser und Luft. Diese Konzentration erlaubt größte Offenheit bei der Planung aller anderen Räume. Außerdem enthält die Powerbox Diele und Treppe, Küche, WC und Bad, einen Abstellraum und optional einen Wellness-Bereich mit Sauna und Fitness-Geräten.

Eine Photovoltaikanlage und thermische Sonnenkollektoren am Dach erzeugen Strom und Wärme. Die Enegiegewinnung ist auch ästhetisch dargestellt, da das komplette Dach aus Photovoltaik besteht. Durch die großflächige Spezialverglasung der Fassade wird die Kraft der Sonne passiv genutzt. Wärmebrückenfreie Dämmung, effiziente Dichtung und Wärmerückgewinnung bei der Lüftung halten die erzeugte Wärme im Haus. Der Sonnenstrom wird ins öffentliche Netz eingespeist.

Plusenergiehaus® generates more power than it consumes. By developing it further to form a modular system, this wooden house with its healthy microclimate can be used even more flexibly: as a detached, semi-detached or terraced house. It can be adapted flexibly to every type of use, room requirement, building plot or land-use plan – with optional extensions, a variable number of storeys, alternative roof forms, and a huge variety of floor plans – even with a lift or as a barrier-free variant.

Thanks to the large variety of modules and a prefabricated »Powerbox«, the construction process is much more efficient. The Powerbox is the command centre for the house's electricity and heat, water and air. Grouping these utilities allows the maximum of freedom when planning all the other rooms. The Powerbox also contains the entrance hall and staircase, the kitchen, toilet and bathroom, a store cupboard and, as an option, a wellness area with a sauna and keep-fit equipment.

Solar cells on the roof and solar panels set at an angle at the edge of the roof generate electricity and heat. As the complete roof is covered with solar cells, this power-generating feature is also aesthetically pleasing. The large-surface special glazing of the façade means the solar energy is also used passively. Insulated to prevent any thermal bridges, and with efficient seals and heat recovery in the ventilation system, the heat that has been generated is kept inside the house. The solar power is fed into the electricity grid.

50

Architektur und Öffentlicher Raum   **Architecture and public space**
Silber   **Silver**

Olympia-Nova   **Sitzelemente**
                   Seating elements

Hersteller / Manufacturer
Erlau AG
D-73431 Aalen

Design / Designer
Werksdesign / In-house design

Ausgewählt insbesondere wegen der Produktinnovation, dass eine Korrosionsbehandlung auf Basis eines natürlichen nachwachsenden Rohstoffes stattfindet, nämlich mit Rilsan®, das aus der Rizinusölpflanze gewonnen wird. Dadurch wird vermieden, dass schädliche Stoffe, wie etwa Lösungsmittel, zum Einsatz kommen. Diese Beschichtung stellt auch bei der Entsorgung kein Problem dar.

Judges panel
Selected especially on the basis of the product innovation that allows corrosion-proofing to be done using a renewable resource: Rilsan®, which comes from the castor bean. This obviates the need for harmful substances such as solvents. The coating does not present any problems when the product is disposed with.

Die Sitzelemente stellen durch die optimierte Rilsan®-Oberflächen-Beschichtung eine umweltfreundliche Produktinnovation dar. Dieser Werkstoff garantiert größte Robustheit und absolute Wartungsfreiheit, einzigartige Hygiene aufgrund seiner bakterienhemmenden Wirkung und eine verblüffende Wärme-/Kälteisolierung.

Rilsan® ist einer der seltenen polymeren Werkstoffe, die aus einer natürlichen Pflanze – aus dem Öl der Rizinuspflanze – und nicht aus einem petrochemischen, künstlichen Grundstoff gewonnen werden. Rilsan® ist damit ein umweltschonender, natürlich vorkommender und nachwachsender Rohstoff. Da die Rilsan®-Oberflächen-Beschichtung ohne Schwermetalle und ohne gesundheitsgefährdende Härter oder Weichmacher hergestellt wird, entsteht zudem bei der Entsorgung kein Sondermüll.

Die Sitzelemente für Park und Fußgängerzone bestehen aus Präzisions-Stahlrohren mit speziell gehärtetem Drahtgitter, die größte Stabilität und Belastbarkeit gewährleisten. Auf den leicht gewölbten Sitzflächen sitzt man leicht federnd, wobei die Spannung nie nachlässt. Durch formal zeitlose und qualitativ hochwertige Gestaltungselemente ist »Olympia-Nova« ein langlebiges Produkt. Dank verschiedenster Sitzelemente ist praktisch jede Sitzkurve und -ecke möglich.

With their optimized surface coating of Rilsan®, these seating elements are an environmentally friendly product innovation. This material is extremely robust, maintenance-free, uniquely hygienic due to its antibacterial properties, and provides surprisingly good insulation against heat and cold.

Rilsan® is one of the few polymeric materials that is made from a plant – in this case the oil from the castor bean – and not from an artificial petrochemical base material. This makes Rilsan® an environmentally friendly, naturally occurring and renewable resource. As the Rilsan® surface coating is made without heavy metals and toxic hardeners or plasticizers, these seating elements can be disposed of without difficulty.

Designed for parks and pedestrian precincts, the seating elements comprise precision tubular steel parts with a specially hardened wire lattice. These guarantee extreme stability and durability. The slightly curved seat surface is slightly springy to sit on, yet always retains its tension. Its formally timeless and high-quality design elements make »Olympia-Nova« a long-lasting product. A wide range of seating elements means that almost any curved or angular arrangement is possible.

TerraZa-Kassette Terrassenbelag
Patio tile

**Architektur und Öffentlicher Raum
Silber**

**Architecture and public space
Silver**

TerraZa-Kassette

**Terrassenbelag
Patio tile**

Hersteller / Manufacturer
Werzalit GmbH + Co. KG
D-71720 Oberstenfeld

Design / Designer
Werksdesign / In-house design
Jörg Golombek

Vertrieb / Distributor
Werzalit GmbH + Co. KG
D-71720 Oberstenfeld

Jury
Das Kompositmaterial aus Kunststoff und Holz verrottet nicht im Außenraum. Werzalit hat angefangen mit diesen Komposits zu arbeiten und sehr schlaue und gut gemachte Produkte daraus entwickelt. Die Terrassenbeläge sind sehr langlebig, veralgen nicht, man rutscht nicht aus, wenn es feucht ist. Es ist noch Holz verarbeitet, aber auf andere Art, auch produktionstechnisch mit größeren Möglichkeiten als mit Reinholz. Ein ökologischer Werkstoff mit einer schönen Farbigkeit. Eine wirklich gute Alternative zu den anderen Terrassenbelägen.

Judges panel
This plastic and wood composite material does not rot outdoors. Werzalit was the first to work with these composite materials, and has developed very clever, well made products out of them. The patio coverings are very long-lasting, algae do not form on their surface, there is no danger of slipping when it is wet. Wood has still been processed here: it is just a different kind of wood, one that has more possibilities than pure wood. An ecological material in attractive colours. A really good alternative to other types of patio coverings.

Das Sortiment von »TerraZa« wurde erweitert: neben dem Profil gibt es nun auch die quadratische »TerraZa«-Kassette. Sie wird ebenso aus einem Holz-Polymerwerkstoff hergestellt, der zu 50 Prozent aus Holz und zu 50 Prozent aus Polypropylen besteht. Da er unbehandelt ist, lässt er sich problemlos recyceln. Einerseits besitzt er alle positiven Eigenschaften von Holz, andererseits ist er in der Verarbeitung formbar und fließfähig wie Thermoplast. So kann »TerraZa« im Spritzgussverfahren hergestellt werden. Aber im Gegensatz zu Holz ist dieser Werkstoff formstabil und beständig gegen Feuchtigkeit und Kälte, Salz- und Chlorwasser, Pilze und Insekten.

Die bewusst schlicht gehaltenen Kassetten bieten neue Gestaltungsmöglichkeiten. Das einfache patentierte Klicksystem erlaubt problemloses Verlegen: längs, quer oder im Wechsel. Somit ergeben sich durch die geriffelte Oberfläche, die »TerraZa« zudem fußfreundlich und rutschfest macht, unterschiedliche interessante Bodenstrukturen.

Die samtige Oberfläche ist in drei naturnahen Farben erhältlich: marrone, terracotta und topino. Die Kassetten sind durch Einarbeiten von Farbpigmenten ganz durchgefärbt und verblassen im Laufe der Zeit ganz natürlich, ohne den farblichen Grundcharakter zu verlieren.

The TerraZa range has been expanded: apart from the long »Profil« sections, there is now also the square »TerraZa« tile. Both are made of a wood-polymer material comprising 50 percent wood and 50 percent polypropylene. As it is untreated, it can be recycled without difficulty. On the one hand, it has all the positive properties of wood, on the other hand it can be formed and is free-flowing during processing, like thermoplast. This means that »TerraZa« can be injection moulded. But unlike wood, this material keeps its shape and is resistant to damp and cold, to brine and chlorinated water, to mould and insects.

The deliberately plain tiles offer new design possibilities. The simple, patented click system makes it simple to lay: with the grooves pointing in one direction, or at right angles to each other. The grooved surface, which also makes »TerraZa« pleasant to walk as well as non-slip, results in different, interesting floor patterns.

The velvet-smooth surface is available in three natural colours: marrone, terracotta and topino. The tiles have been dyed all the way through as a result of pigment added during processing. They fade naturally over the course of time, without losing their basic colour.

54

Architecture and public space
Silver

Touch   **Linoleum Komposit**
Linoleum composite

Hersteller / Manufacturer
Forbo Flooring B.V.
NL-1566 JP Assendelft

Design / Designer
Werksdesign / In-house design
Josee de Pauw, Tamar Gaylord

Vertrieb / Distributor
Forbo Flooring B.V.
NL-1566 JP Assendelft

Jury

Linoleum ist ein Bodenbelag, der sehr ökologisch ist. Das Material ist hervorragend, es ist langlebig, vor allem die gemusterten Varianten. Forbo ist eine herausragende Firma, die immer wieder mit sehr guten neuen Produkten auf den Markt kommt, die Farben sehr schön erneuert und, obwohl das Material bekannt ist und sich über Jahrzehnte behauptet und bewährt hat, trotzdem im Design am Puls der Zeit ist und Neues entwickelt.

Judges panel

Linoleum is a floor covering that is very ecological. The material is excellent. It is long-lasting, especially the patterned versions. Forbo is an outstanding company that repeatedly brings excellent new products onto the market. It is good at giving colours a new lease of life. Although the material is common and has been a stock product for decades, when it comes to design Forbo has its finger on the pulse and comes up with something new.

»Touch« ist ein völlig neuer, innovativer Bodenbelag aus Linoleum und Kork, der aus nachwachsenden Rohstoffen umweltschonend hergestellt wird und ungewöhnliche Gestaltungsmöglichkeiten bietet.

Linoleum wird aus Leinöl, Naturharzen, Holzmehl, Kalksteinfeinmehl und Jute als Trägermaterial gefertigt. Für diesen Werkstoff wurden die Umweltauswirkungen aller Phasen des Produktlebenszyklus – von der Rohstoffgewinnung über Produktion, Transport und Nutzung bis hin zu Recycling und Entsorgung – mit Hilfe einer Lebenszyklus-Analyse (LCA) ermittelt, um ein wirklich nachhaltiges Produkt zu erhalten.

Das Besondere an »Touch« ist, dass es die hygienischen und natürlichen Eigenschaften von Linoleum mit den wohligen und fühlbaren Qualitäten von Kork kombiniert. Damit wurde das altbekannte Linoleum ganz neu interpretiert: Ausgestattet mit haptischen Eigenschaften spricht »Touch« alle Sinne an. Der Bodenbelag hat eine strukturierte, reliefartige Musterung mit subtiler Farbgebung. Die Oberfläche ist sowohl glänzend als auch matt und erscheint erhaben und eben.

»Touch« is a completely new, innovative floor covering made of linoleum and cork. Its production is eco-friendly, using renewable resources, and it offers unusual design possibilities.

Linoleum is made of linseed oil, natural resin, wood flour and powdered limestone, with canvas as a backing material. When developing this material, a life-cycle analysis (LCA) was done to calculate and reduce the environmental impact of every phase of the product life-cycle – from extraction and production of raw materials, via production, transport and use, to recycling and disposal – in order to create a truly sustainable product.

What is special about »Touch« is that it combines the hygienic and natural properties of linoleum with the cosy and tangible qualities of cork. Commonplace linoleum has been completely reinterpreted: with its haptic qualities, »Touch« appeals to all the senses. The floor covering has a structured, raised pattern in subtle colours. The surface is both shiny and matt, and appears to be both embossed and plane.

Focus in Gold

850 kW Windenergieanlage
Wind turbine

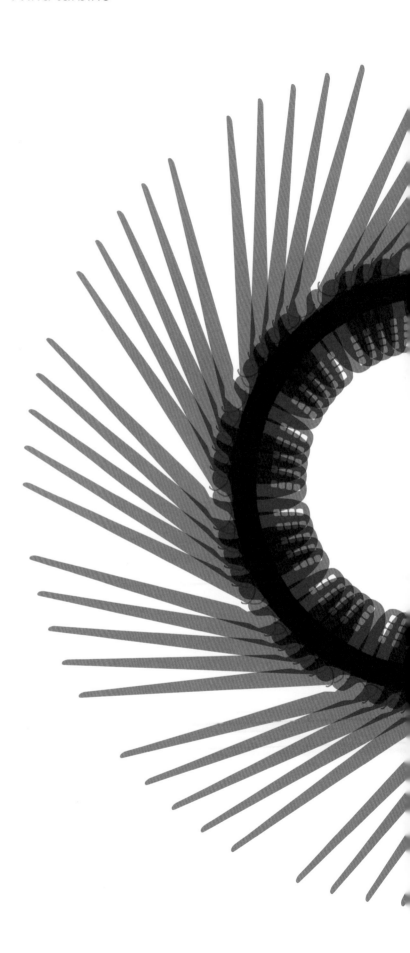

58

Energie- und Gebäudetechnik
Gold

Energy and installations technology
Gold

850kW **Windenergieanlage**
Wind turbine

Hersteller / Manufacturer
Nordwind
Energieanlagen GmbH
D-17033 Neubrandenburg

Design / Designer
Schumann
Büro für industrielle Formentwicklung
D-48167 Münster

Vertrieb / Distributor
Nordwind
Energieanlagen GmbH
D-17033 Neubrandenburg

Jury
Dieses Windrad zeichnet sich dadurch aus, dass es ein neues Getriebe besitzt, das auf hydraulischen Prinzipien aufbaut und insofern sehr viel effizienter, leiser und auch wartungsfreier funktioniert. Darüber hinaus hat sich die Firma auch über ästhetische Aspekte Gedanken gemacht, beispielsweise wie das Windrad durch seine Farbgebung unauffälliger in die Umgebung eingebunden werden kann.

Judges panel
The striking thing about this wind turbine is that it has a new kind of gear unit based on hydraulic principles. This means it works much more efficiently and quietly, and needs less maintenance. In addition, the company has also considered aesthetic aspects, such as how the colour of the wind turbine can help it to harmonize better with its surroundings.

Die Windenergieanlage besitzt eine völlig neuartige Technologie der Energieübertragung. Dabei wird die Kraftübertragung an die Strom erzeugenden Aggregate nicht mehr wie bisher üblich über mechanische Getriebe gelöst, sondern über ein hydrostatisches Pumpensystem. Dieses versorgt zugleich auch andere Funktionskomponenten, wie beispielsweise die Drehantriebe.

Dadurch entfallen viele Verschleißteile sowie interne Energieverbraucher. Das schont nicht nur die Ressourcen und spart Servicekosten, sondern vereinfacht das Handling der Technologie und reduziert die Geräuschbildung, während gleichzeitig der Wirkungsgrad erhöht wird. Dank des zweiflügeligen Rotorkonzeptes sind die Investitionskosten erheblich geringer als bei vergleichbaren Systemen, was den Einsatz der Windenergie fördert.

Die innovativen Aspekte werden durch die Formensprache nach außen kommuniziert. So ist die Anlage kompakter und fügt sich besser in die Landschaft ein. Im Gegensatz zu den sonst sehr pragmatischen und konstruktiven Anlagen wirkt diese Windenergieanlage skulptural und emotional. Damit wurde eine Charakteristik gefunden, die bei allen Leistungs- und somit Größenvarianten der Produkte ein einheitliches Bild ergibt. Die atmosphärische Farbgebung verbindet sich mit den Farbtönen des Himmels und führt zu einer leichten Verschmelzung der beiden Wahrnehmungsebenen.

This wind turbine has a completely new power transmission technology. Instead of conventional mechanical gears, a hydrostatic pump system now transmits power from the rotor blades to the units generating electricity. The system also supplies power to other functional components, such as the drives for turning the blades or nacelle.

This considerably reduces the number of both wear parts and energy consumers. In addition, it not only conserves resources and saves service costs, but also makes the technology easier to handle and quieter, while at the same time it increases the turbine's efficiency. Thanks to its design, with just two rotor blades, the capital cost is considerably lower than for comparable systems, and this encourages the use of wind power.

The turbine's formal expression communicates these innovative features to the observer. The turbine is more compact, for example, and harmonizes better with its surroundings. Compared with other turbines, which are very pragmatic and construction-centred, this wind turbine has a sculptural and emotional feel. This characteristic is common to all the turbines in the series, whatever their output and size. The atmospheric colour scheme blends with the colours of the sky, and causes turbine and sky to merge slightly.

**Energie- und Gebäudetechnik
Silber**

**Energy and installations technology
Silver**

Dali® Multi 3   **Lichtmanagement-System
Light management system**

Hersteller / Manufacturer
Osram GmbH
D-81543 München

Design / Designer
Werksdesign / In-house design

Vertrieb / Distributor
Osram GmbH
D-81543 München

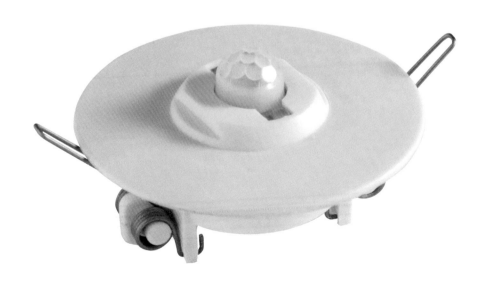

Jury
Der Sinn dieses Sensors ist es, eine bessere, intelligente Steuerung von Licht im Büro oder in anderen großen Räumen zu erreichen. Diese Sensoren sind ja bisher relativ groß und auch nicht besonders hübsch gewesen. Hier hat man versucht, so minimal wie möglich zu gestalten, also wirklich die Technik zu miniaturisieren. Das ist sehr gut gelungen.

Judges panel
The idea of this sensor is to achieve a better, more intelligent control of lighting in offices or other large rooms. Up to now, sensors have been relatively large, and not particularly elegant. Here, the attempt has been made to create as minimalist a design as possible, to really miniaturize the technology. It has certainly succeeded.

Durch steigende Energiepreise und gesetzliche Auflagen wird es immer wichtiger, Lösungen für mehr Energieeffizienz in Bürogebäuden zu erreichen. Dabei spielt das Lichtmanagement eine große Rolle. Steuersysteme, die bedarfsgerecht das zur Verfügung stehende Tageslicht durch Kunstlicht ergänzen sowie die Beleuchtung nur bei anwesenden Personen am Arbeitsplatz einschalten, minimieren den Energieverbrauch.

Das macht »Dali® Multi 3«, ein miniaturisiertes Lichtmanagement-System, das völlig neue Freiräume bietet, Energiesparanwendungen auf kleinstem Raum zu realisieren. Der Deckensensor des Systems hat gerade mal einen Durchmesser von fünf Zentimetern. So lässt er sich überall völlig unauffällig integrieren.

Das Baukastensystem kann flexibel erweitert und sehr vielseitig eingesetzt werden: von der Einzelleuchte bis zum Großraumbüro. Durch die Schwenkbarkeit ist der Erfassungsbereich justierbar. Möglich ist auch seine Fokussierung auf Einzelplätze durch eine aufsteckbare Linse. Das Lichtniveau kann jederzeit individuell eingestellt werden. Es wird sanft abgedimmt, wenn niemand im Erfassungsbereich ist. Hierdurch entstehen keine störende Schalteffekte, die benachbarte Bereiche stören könnten. Mit »Dali® Multi 3« ist es möglich, um bis zu 70 Prozent Strom einzusparen.

With energy prices increasing and legal requirements becoming stricter, it is becoming ever more important to find solutions for more energy efficiency in office buildings. Light management plays an important role here. Energy consumption can be minimized by control systems that provide artificial light as required to supplement the daylight available, and that only switch on lights if people are actually at their desks.

This is where »Dali® Multi 3« comes in, a miniaturized light management system that offers completely new energy-saving applications while taking up a minimum of space. The system's ceiling sensor is just five centimetres in diameter. This means it can be integrated inconspicuously anywhere.

The modular system can be extended flexibly and used in many different ways, from the individual light to the open-plan office. Because it can be swivelled, the area it covers can be adjusted. By attaching a lens, it can also be focused on individual workplaces. The amount of light can be adjusted individually at any time. It is gently dimmed if nobody is within its monitored area. There is therefore no annoying switching on and off of lights that might disturb adjacent areas. »Dali® Multi 3« allows an electricity saving of up to 70 percent.

PT 30k Solar-Inverter
Solar inverter

**Energie- und Gebäudetechnik
Silber**

**Energy and installations technology
Silver**

PT 30k **Solar-Inverter
Solar inverter**

Hersteller / Manufacturer
Sunways AG
Photovoltaic Technology
D-78467 Konstanz

Design / Designer
Melzer-Müller
Industrial Design
CH-8280 Kreuzlingen

Vertrieb / Distributor
Sunways AG
Photovoltaic Technology
D-78467 Konstanz

Jury
Sehr sauber gestaltetes Funktionsprodukt, das seine ökologische Bedeutung durch den Einsatz für Solarenergie hat. Gut gemacht, schöne Oberflächen, sehr funktional. Es ist angenehm zu sehen, dass auch in diesem Nutzbereich Wert darauf gelegt wird, dass die Dinge gut gestaltet sind.

Judges panel
Very neatly designed functional product. Its ecological relevance comes from its use in connection with solar energy. Well made, elegant surfaces, very functional. It is pleasing to see that importance is also placed on well designed objects in a utility area like this.

Der Solar-Inverter besitzt ein zeitlos elegantes kompaktes Gerätedesign. Bei der Auswahl der Komponenten wurde auf Langlebigkeit geachtet – für eine Gerätelebensdauer von bis zu 20 Jahren. Dank dreiphasiger Einspeisung mit bis zu 30 kW Ausgangsleistung auf Basis der bewährten und von Sunways entwickelten HERIC®-Topologie (Highly Efficient & Reliable Inverter Concept) erzielt der »PT 30k« Spitzenerträge und eignet sich besonders für professionelle Photovoltaik-Großanlagen.

Der eigene Energieverbrauch ist im Vergleich zu anderen 30 kW-Geräten minimiert. Der Aufwand an Kabelmaterial wird durch einen dezentralen DC-Anschlusskasten reduziert. Das Gerät ist sehr servicefreundlich. Dank der Sandwichbauweise, die das Gerät beidseitig über Rückseitenblende und Fronttür zugänglich macht, lassen sich die erforderlichen Wartungsarbeiten schneller und kostengünstiger durchführen.

Der »PT 30k« verfügt unter anderem über die neueste CAN-Bus-Technologie zur Vernetzung, über einen integrierten Webserver und über ein aktives Warnsystem. Er zeichnet sich auch durch eine klare, komfortale Bedienerführung auf einem beleuchteten Grafikdisplay mit Tastatur aus.

The design of this compact solar inverter is timelessly elegant. Its components were chosen with a long service life of up to 20 years in mind. Thanks to three-phase feed with up to 30 kW power output, based on the tried and tested HERIC® (highly efficient & reliable inverter concept) topology developed by Sunways, the »PT 30k« achieves top yields, and is especially suitable for professional large-scale photovoltaic systems.

Compared with other 30 kW appliances, it consumes very little electricity itself. The decentralized terminal box means that cable requirements are reduced. The appliance is very easy to service. The sandwich construction allows the appliance to be accessed from the front and the rear, so any necessary maintenance work can be done more rapidly and cost-effectively.

The »PT 30k« also features the latest CAN bus technology, an integrated web server, and an active alarm system. Its illuminated graphic display and keys make it easy and convenient to use.

Vitoladens 300-C Öl-Brennwertkessel
Oil-fired condensing boiler

Energie- und Gebäudetechnik
Silber

Energy and installations technology
Silver

Vitoladens 300-C **Öl-Brennwertkessel**
Oil-fired condensing boiler

Hersteller / Manufacturer
Viessmann Werke GmbH & Co. KG
D-35107 Allendorf

Design / Designer
Phoenix Design
D-70376 Stuttgart

Jury
Ein solides Gerät und eine energieeffizi-
ente Heiztechnik. Gleichzeitig wurde vom
Design her darauf geachtet, dass stan-
dardisierte Teile und pulverbeschichtete
Oberflächen verwendet werden, und
dass die zerlegbare Konstruktion einfach
ist. Die Bedienelemente sind gut mon-
tiert, sodass man sie sehr ergonomisch
bedienen kann.

Judges panel
A sturdy appliance, and energy-efficient
heating technology. At the same time, it
has been designed so that standardized
parts and powder-coated surfaces are
used, and so that it is put together simply
and can be dismantled again. The control elements have been well positioned
so that they can be operated very ergonomically.

Im »Vitoladens 300-C« ist modernste Technik mit
hocheffizienter Brennwerttechnologie integriert. Dabei wird das Energiepotenzial des Brenn-
stoffs Öl nahezu vollständig genutzt, auch die
Kondensationswärme des Wasserdampfes im
Abgas.

Reduziert auf seine wesentliche Funktion, wirt-
schaftlich Wärme ohne Abwärmeverluste zu
erzeugen, sieht das Gerät aus wie ein leistungs-
starker Wärmetresor. Mit seinem völlig klaren
Korpus und der einteiligen Front fügt sich der sil-
berne Öl-Brennwertkessel mit der Akzentfarbe
Orange – Symbol für Wärme – unaufdringlich in
das Umfeld moderner Architektur.

Alle Anschlüsse erfolgen von oben und erlauben
damit eine wandbündige Aufstellung. Unter allen bodenstehenden Öl-Brennwertkesseln hat er
die kompaktesten Abmessungen. Durch den geringen Platzbedarf eignet er sich besonders für
den Austausch von alten Öl-Heizkesseln. Das
Gerät bildet eine Einheit von Technik, Funktion
und Design. Es besitzt eine kompakte Bedienung mit neu entwickeltem User Interface. Der
zweistufige Compact-Blaubrenner passt die
Brennerleistung dem Wärmebedarf an und sorgt
damit für höchste Energieeffizienz.

»Vitoladens 300-C« combines advanced technology with ultra-efficient condensing technology. It
almost completely exploits the energy potential
of the oil that is burned, including the latent heat
of the water vapour in the exhaust gases.

Reduced to its essential function of generating
heat economically without losing heat, the appliance looks like a high performance heat-safe.
With its clear lines and one-part front panel, this
silver oil-fired condensing boiler, with its con-
trasting orange features to symbolize heat, harmonizes perfectly with modern architectural styles.

All connections are made from the top, allowing
the boiler to be mounted flush against the wall.
It is the most compact of all the floor-standing oil-
fired condensing boilers. Since it takes up so
little room, it is ideal when old oil-fired boilers are
being replaced. The appliance forms a unity of
technology, function and design. Its control panel
is compact, with a newly developed user interface. The two-stage compact blue-flame burner
matches its output to actual heat demand, and
so ensures maximum energy efficiency.

Xeoos® PUR white   Kaminofen
Stove

**Energie- und Gebäudetechnik
Silber**

**Energy and installations technology
Silver**

Xeoos® PUR white   **Kaminofen
Stove**

Hersteller / Manufacturer
Specht Modulare Ofensysteme GmbH & Co. KG
D-35116 Hatzfeld

Design / Designer
Global-Mind-Network
D-34117 Kassel

Jury
Ein sehr gutes Produkt. Ausgesprochen innovativ, sowohl ästhetisch als auch von der Nutzung und der Funktion. Optimale Energieausnutzung, auch optisch interessant, weil auf zwei Ebenen Flammen sind.

Judges panel
A very good product. Exceptionally innovative, both aesthetically and in terms of its use and function. Optimum exploitation of energy, also interesting visually because there are flames on two levels.

»Xeoos® PUR white« ist ein Kaminofen, bei dem das Feuer nach oben und unten brennt – dank des weltweit einzigartigen, patentierten Twin-Fire®-Systems. Die Holzscheite werden im oberen Brennraum angezündet. Hat sich ausreichend Glut gebildet, wird durch Starten des TwinFire® ein neuer Weg geöffnet, auf dem der natürliche Schornsteineinzug die Schwelgase durch das heiße Glutzentrum nach unten zieht. Im patentierten mittleren Strömungsboden werden sie bei über 1000°C mit gezielt eingespeister Zuluft vermischt. Das TwinFire® entzündet sich und schließt sich als zweites Feuer an die Glutzone an. Die Asche wirkt als Katalysator: Schadstoffe wie Rauch, Ruß und Kohlenmonoxid werden weitestgehend zu Wasser und Kohlendioxid verbrannt.

Auch bei niedriger Heizleistung herrschen optimale Verbrennungsbedingungen und alle Schwelgase sowie Ruß und Teer werden nahezu vollständig verbrannt. Die gesäuberten Abgase werden unten abgezogen und in den Schornstein geleitet.

Mit dieser innovativen Verbrennungstechnik stößt der Kaminofen bei geringsten Emissionen in Wirkungsgradbereiche um 90 Prozent vor. »Xeoos® PUR white« sticht nicht nur durch sein doppeltes Feuerspiel hervor, sondern auch durch sein klares modernes Design und seine hochwertigen Materialien wie Edelstahl, Aluminium und Glas.

»Xeoos® PUR white« is a stove in which the fire burns upwards and downwards, thanks to the unique, patented TwinFire® system. The logs are lit in the upper combustion chamber. Once there is sufficient heat, TwinFire® is started, opening up a new route for the carbonization gas, which is drawn down through the hot centre of the fire by the natural chimney draft. At a temperature of more than 1000°C in the patented central flow compartment, the gas is mixed with a carefully controlled quantity of additional air. TwinFire® ignites, and a second fire now burns from the ember zone. The ash acts as a catalyst, with the harmful combustion products such as smoke, soot and carbon monoxide being almost completely burned, leaving just water and carbon dioxide.

Even when heat output is low, there is optimum combustion, and all carbonization gases, as well as soot and pitch, are nearly completely burned. The cleansed fumes are drawn down and fed into the chimney.

With this innovative combustion technology, the stove comes close to 90 percent efficiency, combined with minimum emissions. This double fire is not the only striking thing about »Xeoos® PUR white«. It also stands out by virtue of its clear, modern design and its high-quality materials, such as stainless steel, aluminium and glass.

68

**Energie- und Gebäudetechnik
Silber**

**Energy and installations technology
Silver**

UltraSilence® ELS **Einrohrlüftungssystem
Mono-tube ventilation system**

Hersteller / Manufacturer
Helios Ventilatoren GmbH & Co.
D-78056 Villingen-Schwenningen

Design / Designer
Imago Design
D-82064 Straßbach

Vertrieb / Distributor
Helios Ventilatoren GmbH & Co.
D-78056 Villingen-Schwenningen

Jury
Zu Umweltbelastungen gehören auch Lärmbelästigungen. Dieser Ventilator schafft es, mit ganz wenig Geräusch seine Funktion zu erfüllen. Er hat eine niedrige Einbautiefe und ist energieeffizient. Eine schöne Weiterentwicklung der Produkte, die es jetzt auf dem Markt gibt.

Judges panel
Pollution also includes noise pollution. This fan manages to perform its function with very little noise. It is very slim and energy-efficient. An attractive further development of the products that are now available on the market.

»UltraSilence® ELS« wird zur Lüftung innenliegender WCs, Bäder und Küchen mit gewerblicher oder privater Nutzung eingesetzt. Dieses Einrohrlüftungssystem aus langlebigem, recycelbarem Material ist extrem leise – nur 26 Dezibel.

Die ultraflache und minimalistisch gestaltete Fassade, die den Ventilatoreinsatz überdeckt, besticht damit durch ihre unauffällige, zeitlose Eleganz. Ein Präsenzmelder sorgt ganz automatisch bei Betreten des Raumes für eine bedarfsgerechte Lüftung. Mit 0,3 Watt pro m³/h erfüllt »UltraSilence® ELS« neueste Vorgaben der Energieeinsparverordnung.

Außerdem wurden Longlife-Kugellager für 40 000 Betriebsstunden eingesetzt, die wartungsfrei sind. Der Dauerfilter ist sehr großflächig und besitzt eine hohe Schmutzaufnahmekapazität, wodurch die Reinigungsintervalle sehr lang sind. Dann kann er einfach in der Spülmaschine gereinigt werden. Das spart den Kauf teurer Wegwerffilter und schont damit Umweltressourcen ebenso wie der reduzierte Materialeinsatz. So entfällt etwa die Schallisolation durch ein revolutionäres Laufrad in optimierter Aerodynamik, und die Gehäusetiefe ist um 25 Prozent verringert.

»UltraSilence® ELS« is used to ventilate windowless toilets, bathrooms and kitchens, whether used commercially or privately. Made of long-lasting, recyclable materials, this mono-tube ventilation system is extremely quiet – just 26 decibels.

The ultra-flat, minimalist front panel, which covers the fan element, is strikingly elegant: timeless yet unassuming. A sensor ensures that sufficient ventilation is available automatically as soon as someone enters the room. With a power rating of 0.3 W per m³/h, »UltraSilence® ELS« satisfies the latest energy-saving guidelines.

Long-life, maintenance-free bearings have also been used, for up to 40,000 hours of operation. The permanent filter is very generously dimensioned and can trap a great quantity of dust, so that it does not have to be cleaned so frequently. When it does, it is simply put in the dishwasher. This saves having to buy expensive disposable filters. Both this fact and the reduced quantities of materials used to make the fan help conserve resources. A revolutionary impeller with optimized aerodynamics obviates the need for any soundproofing, for example, and the depth of the housing is reduced by 25 percent.

Focus in Gold LED.next »Q64« & »Q36« Deckenleuchtenfamilie
Ceiling light family

Focus in Gold LED.next »Q64« & »Q36« Deckenleuchtenfamilie
Ceiling light family

72

Beleuchtung   Lighting
Gold   Gold

LED.next »Q64« & »Q36«   **Deckenleuchtenfamilie
Ceiling light family**

Hersteller / Manufacturer
Nimbus Group GmbH
D-70469 Stuttgart

Design / Designer
Werksdesign / In-house design
Dietrich Brennenstuhl

Vertrieb / Distributor
Nimbus Group GmbH
D-70469 Stuttgart

Jury
Die Anwendung von LEDs ist eine strom-
sparende Beleuchtungsmöglichkeit.
Hier ist sie sehr ästhetisch umgesetzt,
indem sie in Plexiglas integriert wird
und mit minimalem Abstand zur Decke,
also praktisch direkt auf die Decke, mon-
tiert werden kann. Eine schlichte und
anspruchsvolle Beleuchtungslösung.

Judges panel
LEDs are a source of lighting that saves
electricity. This is a very aesthetic solution
that integrates the LEDs in Plexiglas.
The very thin light is practically mounted
directly on the ceiling. An unassuming
and sophisticated solution.

Ziel war es, Archetypen für die neue LED.next-
Technik zu schaffen. Diese von Nimbus entwickelte
Technologie ist nicht nur ressourcenschonend,
sondern spart gegenüber herkömmlichen Leuchten
50 bis 90 Prozent Energie und hält circa 25 mal
länger. Und nach ihrer extrem langen Lebenszeit
von etwa 50 000 Stunden Brenndauer sind die
Leuchten vollständig recycelbar.

Da es bei dieser innovativen Technologie keine
maßliche Bindung mehr an Komponenten wie
Fassungen und Leuchtmittel gibt, schafft dies einen völlig neuen gestalterischen Freiraum und
ermöglicht ein hochästhetisches, puristisches
Leuchtendesign. Zudem kann sie durch die sehr
geringe Wärmeentwicklung in bisher nicht geeig-
nete, hitzeempfindliche Materialien eingebaut
werden.

Die extrem flache, nur 10 Millimeter hohe Decken-
aufbauleuchte besteht aus einem präzise gefrästen Acryldiffusor, welcher 36 beziehungsweise 64
kegelförmige Bohrungen aufweist, und einer mit
smd-LED bestückten Platine. Die Kombination ist
völlig neuartig und wurde zum Patent angemeldet. Die Deckenleuchten besitzen einfachste Technik, kommen mit einer ungefährlichen 24 Volt
Schutzkleinspannung aus und haben nach dem
Einschalten sofort die volle Lichtleistung.

The aim was to create archetypes for the new
LED.next technology. The technology, developed
by Nimbus, not only conserves resources, but
also uses between 50 and 90 percent less energy
than conventional lights, and lasts roughly 25
times longer. And once their extremely long service life of roughly 50,000 hours is over, the lights
are completely recyclable.

With this innovative technology, there is no longer
any need to take account of the dimensions of
components such as sockets or light bulbs, and
so designers are completely free to create, resulting in a highly aesthetic, puristic design for the
lights. Moreover, because the LEDs generate
very little heat, they can be inserted into heat-sen-
sitive materials that were previously unsuitable.

This extremely flat ceiling light, just 10 millimetres
thick, comprises a precisely milled acrylic diffuser into which 36 or 64 conical holes have been
drilled, and a printed circuit board into which
smd LEDs have been inserted. This combination
is absolutely new, and has been filed for patent.
The ceiling lights work extremely simply on safety
extra low voltage (24 volt), and reach maximum
light output immediately after being switched on.

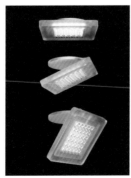

74

Beleuchtung **Lighting**
Silber **Silver**

Office Air LED   **Stehleuchte**
Floorstanding lamp

Hersteller / Manufacturer
Nimbus Group GmbH
D-70469 Stuttgart

Design / Designer
Werksdesign / In-house design
Dietrich Brennenstuhl

Vertrieb / Distributor
Nimbus Group GmbH
D-70469 Stuttgart

Jury
Wenn mehr Menschen mit LEDs und mit ihrer Anwendung im Design experimentieren, entwickeln sich die Werkstoffe sehr viel schneller weiter. Die Stehleuchte ist dafür ein sehr schönes Beispiel. Vorher waren LEDs sehr technisch. Und dies hier ist ein Beweis, dass wir Designer es am besten verstehen, wirklich innovative Produkte zu schaffen.

Judges panel
If more people experiment with LEDs and their design applications, materials develop much faster. This floorstanding lamp is an excellent example. LEDs used to be very technical. This lamp is proof that we designers know best how to create truly innovative products.

Die Stehleuchte »Office Air LED« besteht aus einem extrem flachen, präzise gefrästen Acryldiffusor für direkte Beleuchtung und einem optisch und materiell abgesetzten Kopf für indirekte Beleuchtung.

Die Diffusorplatte besitzt 140 kegelförmige Bohrungen, die das Licht bündeln. Das austretende Licht trifft geneigt und großflächig auf die Tischfläche. Die Diffusorplatte ermöglicht einen blendfreien Arbeitsbereich – ideal für Bildschirmarbeitsplätze.

Durch die von Nimbus weiterentwickelte LED.next-Technik konnte der Wirkungsgrad der klassischen Arbeitsplatzleuchte nachhaltig verbessert werden. Einerseits lässt sich dank der gerichteten Lichtabgabe der LEDs, die direkt auf die Arbeitsfläche strahlen, der Stromverbrauch im Vergleich zu Leuchtstofflampen um bis zu 50 Prozent senken. Andererseits ist es erstmalig möglich, ausschließlich das direkte Arbeitsplatzlicht zu schalten und damit weitere 60 Prozent Energie zu sparen. Ein weiterer Vorteil: die hohe Leuchtmittellebensdauer von 50 000 Stunden.

The »Office Air LED« floorstanding lamp comprises an extremely flat, precisely milled acrylic diffuser for direct lighting. The top of the diffuser, for indirect lighting, is made of a different material, and so contrasts with the bottom half.

140 conical holes, which focus the light, have been drilled into the diffuser plate. The light which is emanated hits the desk top at an angle, and over a large surface. The diffuser plate provides a glare-free workspace –ideal when working at a monitor.

Nimbus has developed LED.next technology further, allowing a sustained improvement to the efficiency of the classic desk lamp. First, because the light from the LEDs is guided directly onto the work surface, energy consumption is as much as 50 percent less than with fluorescent lamps. Second, this is the first time that the workplace light alone can be switched on, allowing a further energy saving of 60 percent. One further advantage is the long life of the LEDs, which last for 50,000 hours.

Beleuchtung   Lighting
Silber   Silver

Geldsparleiste® MoneySaver   **Abschaltbare Steckerleiste
Disconnectable multipoint connector**

Hersteller / Manufacturer
Zweibrüder Optoelectronics GmbH
D-42699 Solingen

Design / Designer
Werksdesign / In-house design
Stefan Feustel, Harald Opolka

Vertrieb / Distributor
Zweibrüder Optoelectronics GmbH
D-42699 Solingen

Jury
Das Produkt spart Energie. Das Problem ist erkannt und eine sehr gute Lösung gefunden: Steckerleiste und Schalter sind getrennt. Denn oft ist man zu bequem, um bei der herkömmlichen Steckerleiste unter den Tisch zu kriechen, um auszuschalten. Hier dagegen: Einfach auf den Fußschalter treten und alles ist aus. Das Prinzip ist toll.

Judges panel
This product saves energy. The problem has been recognized, and an excellent solution found. The connector and the switch are separate. With conventional multipoint connectors, we are often too lazy to crawl under the table and switch them off. All you have to do here is step on the switch, and everything is off. A super idea.

Viele Elektrogeräte haben nicht nur im Standby-Modus, sondern selbst wenn sie komplett ausgeschaltet sind einen hohen Stromverbrauch. Bei der Erzeugung einer Kilowattstunde elektrischer Energie entstehen etwa 0,6 Kilogramm Kohlendioxid. Durch Standby und andere Leerlaufverluste werden jährlich in Deutschland rund acht Millionen Tonnen Kohlendioxid freigesetzt.

Im Gegensatz zu herkömmlichen Steckerleisten trennt der »MoneySaver« alle Adern vom Netz. Damit sind die Geräte gleichzeitig vor Spannungsspitzen und Blitzschlägen geschützt.

Mit der Geldsparleiste® »MoneySaver« lassen sich bis zu sechs Elektrogeräte bequem, selbst wenn die Steckerleiste hinter Schränken, Kommoden oder Schreibtischen verborgen ist, durch einen leichten Fußdruck auf den externen Fußschalter an- und abschalten. Eine kleine Kontrollleuchte im Fußschalter zeigt an, ob noch Geräte am Netz sind.

Die Steckerleiste kann mit Haltebändern an Schreibtischbeinen oder mit der integrierten Wandhalterung direkt an der Wand befestigt werden. Mit dem »MoneySaver«, der auch eine Kindersicherung besitzt, kann man Strom und Geld sparen und damit die Umwelt schonen und zum Klimaschutz beitragen.

Many electrical appliances consume a lot of electricity not only in stand-by mode, but even when they have been switched off altogether. The generation of one kilowatt-hour of electricity creates roughly 0.6 kilograms of carbon dioxide. In Germany, stand-by and other idling losses cause annual CO_2 emissions of roughly eight million tons.

Unlike conventional multipoint connectors, the »MoneySaver« disconnects all leads from the mains. This also protects appliances from power surges and lightning.

Even if the »MoneySaver« is hidden behind cupboards or desks, light pressure on the external foot switch is all that is needed to connect or disconnect up to six electrical appliances. A small display light in the foot switch shows whether appliances are still connected to the mains.

The connector can also be attached to desk legs by means of straps, or attached directly to the wall by means of the integrated wall bracket. The »MoneySaver«, which is also childproof, allows money and electricity to be saved, and thus helps protect the environment and the climate.

Focus in Gold

e-motion   Zusatzantrieb für manuelle Rollstühle
Auxiliary motor for manual wheelchairs

80

Medizin und Rehabilitation
Gold

Medicine and rehabilitation
Gold

e-motion   **Zusatzantrieb für manuelle Rollstühle**
Auxiliary motor for manual wheelchairs

Hersteller / Manufacturer
Ulrich Alber GmbH
D-74361 Albstadt

Design / Designer
Einmaleins
Büro für Gestaltung
D-88483 Burgrieden

Vertrieb / Distributor
Ulrich Alber GmbH
D-74361 Albstadt

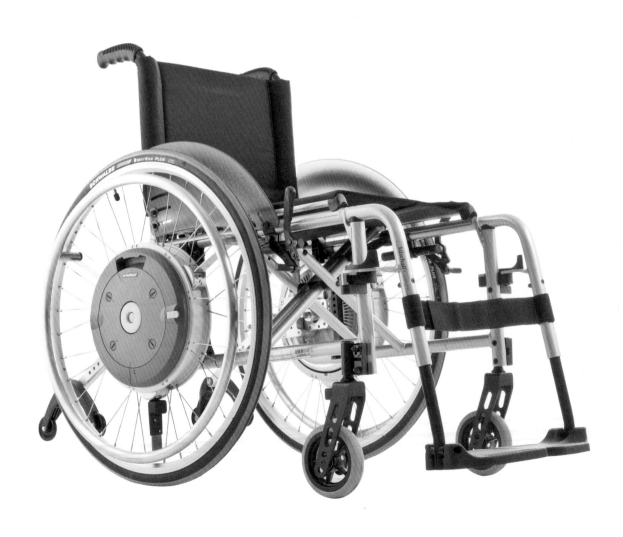

Jury
Hervorragendes Produkt, weil nahezu jeder konventionelle Rollstuhl mit diesem dezenten, kleinen Elektroantrieb aufgerüstet werden kann. Eine exemplarisch gute Lösung für mitwachsende Produkte, Reduzierung von Bauteilen, von Komponenten und von Produkten. Und es sieht auch noch gut aus. Die Lebensqualität wird gesteigert, weil sich Rollstuhlfahrer damit leichter fortbewegen können. Man ist immer noch aktiv, auch wenn man vielleicht nicht mehr so kräftig ist.

Judges panel
An excellent product, because nearly every conventional wheelchair can be fitted with this unassuming, small electric motor. A good example of a product that grows with the user, of how to reduce the number of parts, components and products. And it looks good, too. Quality of life is enhanced, because the wheelchair-user can move around more easily. The user is still active, even though he may no longer be so strong.

»e-motion« ist eine ideale Synthese aus fortschrittlicher, wirtschaftlicher und umweltschonender Rehabilitationstechnik, die Rollstuhlfahrern ein selbstbestimmtes und aktives Leben ermöglicht. Der nachrüstbare elektrische Zusatzantrieb für manuelle Rollstühle, der in den Radnaben integriert wird, verbindet aktive Mobilität mit therapeutischem Nutzen. Er unterstützt die Anschubbewegung des Rollstuhlfahrers, der in Bewegung bleibt und so seine Vitalfunktionen trainiert.

Die Gesamtkonstruktion ist auf Haltbarkeit und mehrfachen Einsatz ausgelegt. Dank einer marktüblichen Steckachse und wenigen Befestigungsteilen kann der Zusatzantrieb mit fast allen manuellen Rollstühlen kombiniert sowie schnell und kostengünstig an den neuen Anwender und dessen Rollstuhl angepasst werden.

»e-motion« ist so konstruiert, dass er an seinem Produktlebensende mit einfachen Mitteln sortenrein zerlegt werden kann. Auf Einsatz von Verbundstoffen wurde verzichtet. Alle Kunststoffmaterialien können recycelt werden. Alle Elektronikbauteile sind in umweltschonender, bleifreier Technik ausgeführt und entsprechen bereits heute zukünftigen Standards. Dank neuartiger Wickeltechnologie enthält der Antrieb nur noch 35 Prozent der Kupfermenge des Vorgängermodells. »e-motion« ist nicht nur effizienter, sondern seine Akkus sind durch die für diesen Produktbereich völlig neu entwickelte Lithium-Ionen-Technologie wesentlich länger haltbar.

»e-motion« is an ideal synthesis of advanced, economical and environmentally friendly rehabilitation technology, which allows wheelchair users an independent and active life. This electric auxiliary motor can be fitted to manual wheelchairs by integrating it in the wheel hub. It combines active mobility with therapeutic benefit. It supports the wheelchair user as he pushes the wheel forward. In this way, the user remains active, and trains his vital functions.

The overall design is geared to durability and reuse. As it uses a conventional full-floating axle and just a few mounting parts, the auxiliary motor can be combined with nearly every manual wheelchair, and adjusted quickly and cost-effectively to the new user and his wheelchair.

»e-motion« is designed in such a way that it can easily be broken down into its individual materials at the end of its useful life. No composite materials have been used in its construction. All the plastic materials can be recycled. All the electronic components are lead-free, and thus environmentally friendly, and already comply with future standards. Thanks to an innovative winding technology, the motor contains only 35 percent as much copper as its predecessor model. »e-motion« is not only more efficient, but its rechargeable batteries last considerably longer, thanks to the completely new lithium-ion technology developed for this product area.

82

Medizin und Rehabilitation   Medicine and rehabilitation
Silber   Silver

Shock-Proof   **Blutdruckmessgerät**
              Blood pressure instrument

              Hersteller / Manufacturer
              Rudolf Riester GmbH & Co. KG
              D-72417 Jungingen

              Design / Designer
              RED Research Engineering Design
              D-70182 Stuttgart

              Vertrieb / Distributor
              Rudolf Riester GmbH & Co. KG
              D-72417 Jungingen

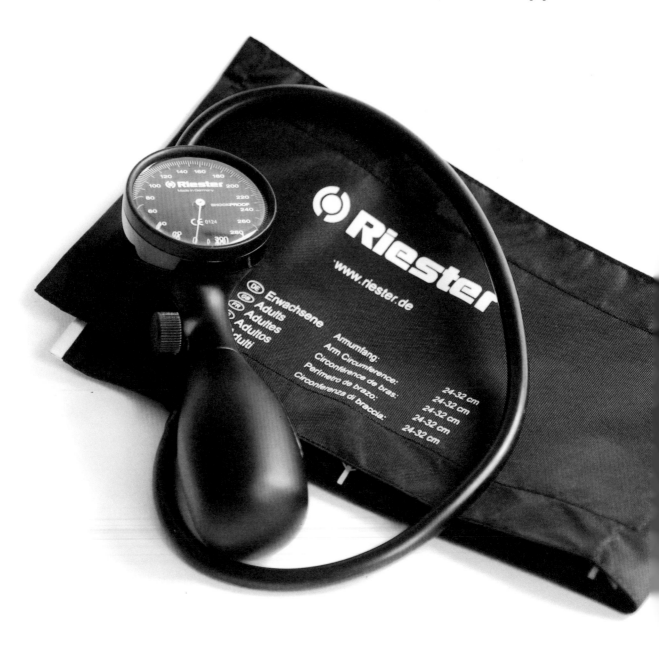

Jury
Typische Strategie der Lebensdauerver-
längerung. Dadurch, dass das Produkt
robuster gestaltet ist, ist es auch sicherer,
es kann nicht so leicht beschädigt werden, man liest nicht falsch ab. Longlife-
Design, ökologisch sehr sinnvoll.

Judges panel
Typical service life-prolongation strategy.
Making the product more robust also
makes it safer. It cannot be damaged so
easily, and readings are not false. Long-
life design, makes a lot of sense ecologically.

Das Blutdruckmessgerät »Shock-Proof« zeichnet
sich durch lebenslange zuverlässige Blutdruck-
messung aus. Das gelang dank der innovativen
»Shock-Proof«-Technologie, die mit der Fraunhofer TEG entwickelt wurde.

Bei herkömmlichen Geräten sind bei einem Sturz
oder sonstiger grober Handhabung exakte und
zuverlässige Messungen nicht mehr möglich. An-
ders bei »Shock-Proof«: Das Gerät besitzt eine
innovative Dämpfung, die dem harten Klinikein-
satz standhält. Damit bietet es sehr lange Zeit
exakte Messungen. Blutdruckmessgeräte müssen somit nicht mehr regelmäßig ersetzt werden, was nicht nur ein ökonomischer Vorteil ist,
sondern letztendlich auch Ressourcen und Umwelt schont.

Das Gerät ist sehr bedienerfreundlich: Das spezielle Löffel- und Balldesign ermöglicht ein schnel-
les Aufpumpen und Ablassen der Luft. Der ergonomisch geformte Griff liegt gut in der Hand und
die Skala ist sehr übersichtlich gestaltet.

The »Shock-Proof« blood pressure instrument
provides reliable blood pressure readings across
the span of an entire lifetime. It can do so thanks
to the innovative »Shock-Proof« technology developed together with the Fraunhofer Technology
Development Group (TEG).

If they are dropped or treated roughly in some
other way, conventional instruments can no
longer provide exact and reliable readings. With
»Shock-Proof«, it is a different story. The instrument features an innovative damping system
that can withstand the kind of rough treatment
that is common in hospital use. It can therefore
provide exact readings for an extremely long
time. This means that blood pressure instruments
no longer have to be replaced regularly, which
is not only an economic advantage but, in the end,
also conserves resources and protects the environment.

The instrument is very easy to use: the special
spoon and ball design allows it to be quickly inflated and deflated. The ergonomically shaped
handle fits snugly into the hand, and the measuring scale is very clearly set out.

84

Medizin und Rehabilitation
Silber

Medicine and rehabilitation
Silver

Portello   Daumen-Orthese
Thumb orthosis

Hersteller / Manufacturer
Christina Weskott
Finger- und Handorthesen
D-50858 Köln

Design / Designer
Werksdesign / In-house design

Vertrieb / Distributor
Christina Weskott
Finger- und Handorthesen
D-50858 Köln

Eine Innovation in der Orthopädie stellt die Dau-
menorthese aus Sterlingsilber dar. Dieses medi-
zinische Hilfsmittel wird eingesetzt bei Verschleiß
im Daumensattelgelenk und Instabilität des
Daumengrundgelenkes. Hauptsymptom ist der
Schmerz, und es entwickelt sich eine Fehlstel-
lung des Daumens. Bei der Therapie steht die
Schmerzreduzierung zusammen mit der Korrektur
des Daumens im Mittelpunkt.

Im Gegensatz zu herkömmlichen Orthesen sitzt
»Portello« ohne Befestigungsmechanik am Handgelenk direkt am Daumen, der damit beweglich
bleibt. Alle Arbeiten – im Haushalt, im Büro, am
PC, im Garten – können problemlos ausgeführt
werden. »Portello« korrigiert und stabilisiert das
defekte Daumengelenk und bewirkt Schmerz-
linderung. Ein Fortschreiten der Daumendeformie-
rung wird verhindert.

Die Schiene ist materialbeständig, hygienisch
und recycelbar. Außerdem sieht es nicht wie ein or-
thopädisches Produkt, sondern wie ein Schmuck-
stück aus. »Portello« verbindet Funktionalität
mit hochwertiger Verarbeitung und klarer attrak-
tiver Formensprache.

This sterling-silver thumb orthosis is an innovation
in orthopaedic treatment. It is used in cases of
saddle-joint arthrosis and instability of the thumb
base joint. This condition is extremely painful,
and leads to a false position of the thumb. Treatment focuses on relieving pain and correcting
the position of the thumb.

Unlike conventional orthotic devices, »Portello«
needs no fixation, but rests on the wrist directly at
the thumb, which thus remains movable. Work
in the household, in the office, at the PC or in the
garden can be done without difficulty. »Portello«
corrects and stabilizes the defective thumb joint,
and helps to relieve pain. It prevents any worsen-
ing of the deformation of the thumb.

The orthosis is made of long-lasting material, and
is hygienic and recyclable. Moreover, it does not
look like an orthopaedic product at all, but like a
piece of jewellery. »Portello« combines functionality with high-quality workmanship and clear, attractive formal expression.

MarLED OP-LED-Leuchte
LED surgery light

Medizin und Rehabilitation
Silber

Medicine and rehabilitation
Silver

MarLED **OP-LED-Leuchte**
LED surgery light

Hersteller / Manufacturer
Karl-Leibinger Medizintechnik
D-78570 Mühlheim

Design / Designer
Weinberg & Ruf
Produktgestaltung
D-70794 Filderstadt

Vertrieb / Distributor
Karl-Leibinger Medizintechnik
D-78570 Mühlheim

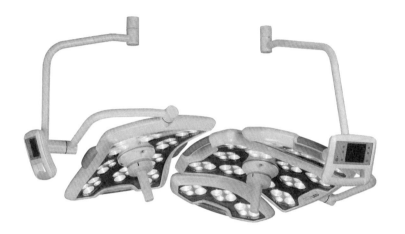

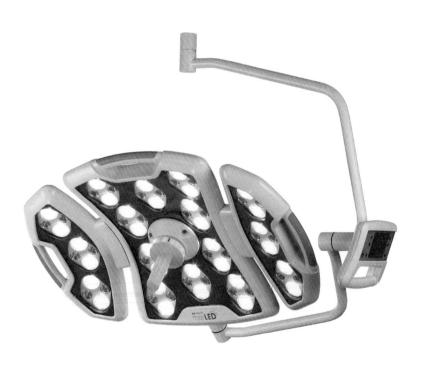

Die OP-Leuchten zeichnen sich durch einen licht-
technisch neuartigen Ansatz und raumsparen-
des Design aus. Ein radikal neues Reflektoren- und
Gehäusekonzept unterstützt den Chirurgen bei
seiner Arbeit nachhaltig.

In den OP-Leuchten werden Hochleistungs-LEDs
für die Beleuchtung selbst schwierigster OP-Si-
tuationen eingesetzt. Diese neueste LED-Technik
sorgt nicht nur für Langlebigkeit und Energieeffizienz, sondern bietet auch ungeahnte Schatten-
freiheit und Farbtreue. Für die optimale Anpas-
sung an das tatsächliche OP-Feld kann das be-
leuchtete Feld jetzt nicht nur kreisförmig sondern auch länglich eingestellt werden. Die kompakte und flache Form der Leuchte erleichtert
die Positionierung über dem OP-Tisch und sorgt
für eine bessere Ausleuchtung.

Das Design passt sich hervorragend in das tech-
nikbetonte Umfeld eines OP-Saales ein. Eine klare
Linienführung verzichtet auf scharfe Ecken und
Kanten, um Verletzungen der Operateure zu ver-
meiden. Die glatten Oberflächen und stufen-
losen Formübergänge erleichtern die Reinigung.
Dank der ergonomisch gestalteten und in die
Form integrierten Griffe lässt sich die Leuchte
leicht handhaben und positionieren.

These surgery lights stand out by virtue of their
novel lighting technology and space-saving
design. A radically new reflector and housing concept makes the surgeon's work easier.

The surgery lights use high-power LEDs to illu-
minate even the most difficult surgical situations.
This latest LED technology is not only long-lasting and energy-efficient, but also provides unpre-
cedented shadow reduction and true-colour
rendition. For the best possible adjustment to the
actual area under surgery, the illuminated area
can be set to be not only circular, but also rectangular. The compact, flat form of the light makes
it easier to position it over the operating table, and
provides better illumination.

The design harmonizes excellently with the technical environment of an operating theatre. Its
clear lines do without sharp corners and edges,
and in this way prevents injury to surgical per-
sonnel. The smooth surfaces and joints make
it easier to clean. Thanks to the ergonomically
shaped, integrated handle, the light is easy to
handle and position.

Raindance® Duschsystem
Connect Showerpipe EcoSmart   Shower system

Bad und Sanitär
Silber

Bathrooms and sanitary installations
Silver

Raindance® Connect Showerpipe EcoSmart

Duschsystem
Shower system

Hersteller / Manufacturer
Hansgrohe AG
D-77761 Schiltach

Design / Designer
Phoenix Design
D-70376 Stuttgart

Vertrieb / Distributor
Hansgrohe Deutschland
Vertriebs GmbH
D-77761 Schiltach

Jury
Die große Fläche der Brause ermöglicht
eine gute Reinigung. Das Duschsystem
hat eine Dosierung, man verbraucht ganz
wenig Wasser. Die Kopfbrause oben
und die Handbrause bieten zusammen
eine wunderbare Dusche. Schön, ökologisch und kompromisslos. Das sieht man
kaum unter den ökologischen Produkten,
die es auf dem Markt gibt.

Judges panel
The shower head's large surface area
makes it easy to clean. The shower system meters water. Very little water is
used. The combination of hand-held and
overhead shower creates a wonderful
shower experience. Beautiful, ecological
and uncompromising. In the ecological products that are on the market, this
is not something you see very often.

Das Duschsystem besteht aus einer Kopfbrause
und einer Handbrause. Um die Kopfbrause zu
aktivieren, steckt man einfach die Handbrause in
den Rain Connector®, und das Wasser wird automatisch durch die Brausestange geführt. Um-
stellen ist nicht nötig. Die Kopfbrause bietet einen großflächigen Brauseregen, der den Körper
in einen »Wassermantel« einhüllt.

Dank einer speziellen Durchflussregulierung im
Innern der Brause liegt ihr Wasserverbrauch mit
9,5 Litern pro Minute deutlich unter dem einer
konventionellen Tellerkopfbrause. Ein sich verfor-
mender Präzisions-O-Ring reagiert auf die Höhe
des Fließdrucks, sodass die verbrauchte Wassermenge unabhängig von den Druckverhältnis-
sen nahezu gleich bleibt. Zugleich wird die Strahlfunktion an die Wassermenge angepasst, damit
der Duschkomfort nicht leidet. Die Verwirbelung
von Luft und Wasser im Innern der Brause sorgt
für einen satten Regen weicher Tropfen.

Das Duschsystem zeichnet sich durch sein klares
und puristisches Design aus und lässt sich ohne
aufwändigen Umbau in jedes Bad installieren, in
dem bereits eine Handbrause vorhanden ist.

This shower system comprises a fixed and a hand-
held shower head. To activate the fixed shower
head, the hand-held shower head is simply inserted into the Rain Connector®, and water is
automatically fed through the shower rail. There
is no need to turn any levers. The fixed shower
head provides a wide-area shower that envelops
the body in a »water coat«.

Thanks to a special flow control inside the shower
head, it consumes only 9.5 litres a minute – far
less than a conventional overhead shower. A duc-
tile precision O-ring reacts to the amount of
flow pressure, with the result that the quantity
of water used remains almost constant, regard-
less of pressure level. At the same time, the jet is
adjusted to the amount of water, so that there is
no loss of shower comfort. Mixing air to agitate
the water inside the shower head creates a rich
shower of soft droplets.

The shower system stands out by virtue of its
clear, purist design, and can be installed in any
bathroom without extensive modifications. All
that is needed is an already existing hand-held
shower.

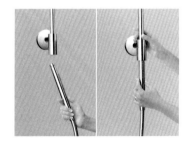
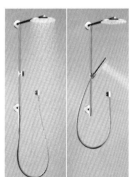

90

Bad und Sanitär
Silber

Bathrooms and sanitary installations
Silver

Crometta® 85 Green   **Handbrause**
Hand-held shower

Hersteller / Manufacturer
Hansgrohe AG
D-77761 Schiltach

Design / Designer
Phoenix Design
D-70376 Stuttgart

Vertrieb / Distributor
Hansgrohe Deutschland Vertriebs GmbH
D-77761 Schiltach

Jury
Es ist eine wassersparende Duschar-
matur, sehr effizient, weil sie nur sechs
Liter Wasser pro Minute verbraucht. Und
das ist, ökologisch gesehen, sehr schön.
Klassisches, langlebiges Design.

Judges panel
This is a water-saving shower fitting, very
efficient, because it only uses six litres
per minute. From an ecological point of
view, that is very good. Classic, long-
lasting design.

Die neu entwickelte EcoSmart-Technologie reduziert den Wasserverbrauch der »Crometta® 85
Green« um bis zu 60 Prozent im Vergleich zu herkömmlichen Brausen. Eine Kombination aus
ausgeklügelter Durchflussregulierung und zen-
traler Luftansaugung ermöglicht einen maxi-
malen Wasserverbrauch von nur sechs Litern pro
Minute.

Die Strahlfunktion passt sich unabhängig vom
Wasserdruck automatisch der Wassermenge an,
gibt die gewünschte Kraft und senkt den Wasserverbrauch. Dabei ist stets ein angenehmer Duschkomfort gewährleistet, zumal das Wasser-Luft-
Gemisch dem Strahl trotz reduzierten Wasserver-
brauchs die nötige Power für echten Duschspaß
verleiht. So werden wertvolle Wasser- und – da in
der Regel mit warmem Wasser geduscht wird
– Energieressourcen geschont.

Dank ihres schlichten und zeitlosen Designs eignet sich die Wasser- und Energiesparbrause sehr
gut für den unkomplizierten Austausch in vorhandenen Bädern.

The newly developed EcoSmart technology reduces the water consumption of »Crometta® 85
Green« by as much as 60 percent compared with
conventional shower heads. A combination of sophisticated flow control and central air suction
allows a maximum water consumption of just six
litres a minute.

The jet function adapts automatically to water
volume, independently of water pressure, providing the power that is desired while reducing
water consumption. Pleasant shower comfort is
always guaranteed, especially as the air-water
mixture always provides the power needed for
real shower fun, despite the reduction in water
consumption. This means that valuable water is
saved, and – since most people take hot showers
– energy resources as well.

Thanks to its pure, timeless design, this water and
energy-saving shower head can easily replace
existing fittings when bathrooms are renovated.

Bad und Sanitär
Silber

Bathrooms and sanitary installations
Silver

Eva Solo   **Seifenspender**
Soap dispenser

Hersteller / Manufacturer
Eva Denmark A/S
DK-2760 Måløv

Design / Designer
Tools Design®
Claus Jensen & Henrik Holbæk
DK-2400 Kopenhagen NV

Vertrieb / Distributor
Eva Denmark A/S
DK-2760 Måløv

Jury
Manchmal müssen Dinge einfach nur schön sein, damit sie genutzt werden. Gleichzeitig reduziert man damit Kunststoffmüll und Transportaufwand. Und man kann sich jeden Morgen im Bad an einem wirklich hervorragend gestalteten Gegenstand freuen und geht vielleicht positiver in den Tag.

Judges panel
Some things only have to be beautiful for them to be used. At the same time, this is a product that reduces plastic waste and transport costs. And every morning, the user can take pleasure in a truly excellently designed object, and may start the day better on the strength of it.

Der Seifenspender kann – gefüllt mit flüssiger Handseife oder Shampoo – in Bad und Toilette eingesetzt werden. Er lässt sich aber genauso gut in der Küche neben der Spüle verwenden, wenn man ihn mit Spülmittel füllt.

Er ersetzt Kunststoffseifenspender, die nur einmal verwendet und anschließend weggeworfen werden. Somit wird Müll reduziert, was wiederum die Umwelt schont.

Mit seiner eleganten, schlichten, minimalistischen Gestaltung mit stromlinienförmigen weichen Rundungen und seinem hochwertigen Material – Edelstahl – bietet der Seifenspender einen schönen Blickfang: ein langlebiges Produkt. Man dosiert Seife oder Spülmittel, indem man einfach leicht auf die Kappe drückt.

After filling with liquid soap or shampoo, this soap dispenser can be used in the bathroom or toilet. But it can equally well be used next to the sink in the kitchen if it is filled with washing-up liquid.

It can be used instead of plastic soap dispensers that are used just once and then thrown away. This reduces waste, which in its turn protects the environment.

It is elegant, pure and minimalistic in design, with streamlined, soft rounded edges. This design, together with the high-quality stainless steel the dispenser is made of, makes it a joy to behold. It is a long-lasting product. Soap or washing-up liquid are dispensed simply by applying light pressure to the lid.

96

Catering Kitchen **Die mobile Küche**
The mobile kitchen

Hersteller / Manufacturer
Eisfink Max Maier GmbH & Co. KG
D-71636 Ludwigsburg

Design / Designer
Pearl Creative GmbH
Tim Storti, Christian Rummel, Max Maier
D-71636 Ludwigsburg

Vertrieb / Distributor
Eisfink Max Maier GmbH & Co. KG
D-71636 Ludwigsburg

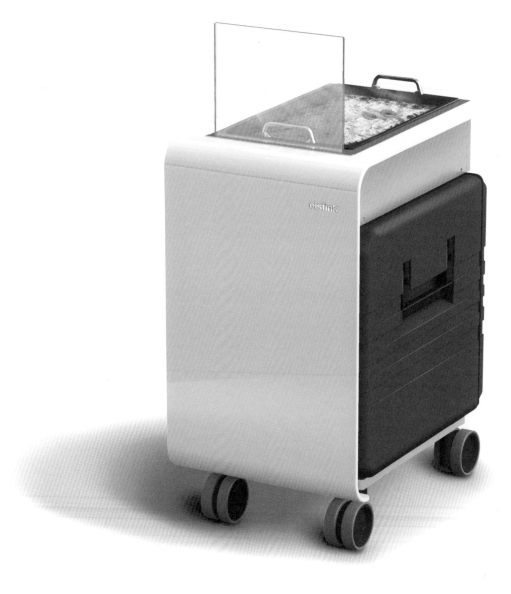

Jury
Gelungenes Design. Es ist sehr schlicht, es ist durchdacht, die Modularität ist überzeugend und gleichzeitig kommt der ökologische Aspekt dazu, dass hier ein Sandwichmaterial eingesetzt wird, das von der Wärmeübertragung und von der Effizienz besonders gut ist. Sehr schlau und ausgezeichnet.

Judges panel
Nicely designed. It is very unostentatious and well thought-through. Its modular construction makes sense, and then there is the ecological aspect of the sandwich material used, which is an especially good transmitter of heat and is very efficient. Very clever. Excellent.

Die mobile Küche kann flexibel und vielseitig vom Einzelmodul bis zur kompletten Küchenzeile verwendet werden. Dabei lässt sie sich sehr leicht auf- und abbauen. Alle Teile werden nur aufeinandergestellt und gesteckt verbunden – Schrauben oder zusätzliche Verbindungsteile entfallen.

Dank der selbsttragenden Speisentransportbehälter konnte auf zusätzliche Rahmenkonstruktionen und Möbelelemente verzichtet werden, was den Materialeinsatz auf ein Minimum reduziert und Ressourcen schont. Zudem wurden ausschließlich hochwertige Materialien, wie leicht recycelbare Edelstähle und sehr belastbare Kunststoffe eingesetzt, die die »Catering Kitchen« zu einem robusten und langlebigen System machen. Dafür sorgt auch das zeitlose Design: funktional, ästhetisch und schlicht.

Mit den Küchenkomponenten aus Varithek®, Thermoplates® und Thermoport® werden in allen Bereichen der Zubereitung Energieverluste minimiert. Die aus dem patentierten Mehrschichtmaterial für optimale Wärmeübergänge Swissply® gefertigten Thermoplates® – Kochtöpfe in Gastronorm-Format – revolutionieren den Foodflow: lagern, kühlen, vorbereiten, kochen, grillen, transportieren und ausgeben aus einem Behältnis. Umfüllschritte entfallen, was den Reinigungsaufwand reduziert. Im Energiesafe Thermoport® werden die Speisen über lange Zeit wirkungsvoll warm oder kühl gehalten ohne zusätzliche Energie zu benötigen.

The mobile kitchen can be used flexibly and in a variety of ways, from a stand-alone module to a complete kitchen. It can be assembled and disassembled very easily. All the parts are simply placed on top of each other and plugged together, with no need for screws or additional ties.

Thanks to the self-supporting food transport container, there was no need for any additional framework construction or furniture elements, and this reduces the use of materials to a minimum and conserves resources. In addition, only high-quality materials have been used, such as easily recyclable stainless steel and extremely tough plastic. They make the Catering Kitchen a sturdy, long-lasting system. This long-lasting quality is underlined by the timeless design, which is functional, aesthetic and unassuming.

With kitchen components made of Varithek®, Thermoplates® and Thermoport®, energy loss is minimized at every stage of food preparation. The Thermoplates® saucepans, made of patented Swissply®, a multilayer material that allows optimum transmission of heat, comply with the gastronorm standard. This revolutionizes the food flow: in one and the same vessel, food can be stored, cooled, cooked, grilled, transported, and served. There is no need to transfer the food to a new container, which reduces the need for cleaning. In the Thermoport® energy safe, food is efficiently kept hot or cold over a long period without the need for additional energy.

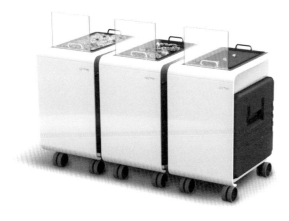

Hausgeräte
Silber

Household appliances
Silver

W 1749 WPS LiquidWash   **Waschmaschine**
Washing machine

Hersteller / Manufacturer
Miele & Cie. KG
D-33332 Gütersloh

Design / Designer
Werksdesign / In-house design
Andreas Enslin

Vertrieb / Distributor
Miele & Cie. KG
D-33332 Gütersloh

Jury
Die Waschmaschine hat die üblichen guten Qualitäten, die man von Miele kennt, mit einer automatischen, elektronischen Steuerung, mit Erkennung des Befüllungsgrades. Zusätzlich hat sie einen Spender für Waschmittel, der automatisch dosiert, das heißt man kann nicht mehr überdosieren, es wird effizient mit dem Waschmittel umgegangen. Ungewöhnliches Design, das sich durch eine interessante Linienführung auszeichnet und aus dem Markt der sehr gleichen Haushaltsgeräte hervorsticht.

Judges panel
This washing machine has the usual good properties we have come to expect from Miele, with automatic electronic control and a load measuring function. In addition, it has a dispenser for detergent that automatically gauges the quantity required. It is no longer possible to add too much: detergent is used efficiently. Unusual design with interesting lines. In a market in which these household appliances are very similar, this washing machine stands out.

Bei der »W 1749 WPS LiquidWash« wird das Flüssigwaschmittel, das sich in einem transparenten Behälter auf der Waschmaschine befindet, automatisch dosiert. Das ist möglich dank einer Beladungserkennung und einer Dosierpumpe. Der Nutzer muss nur noch das gewünschte Waschprogramm und den jeweiligen Verschmutzungsgrad der Wäsche einstellen.

Da die Dosierung immer bedarfsgenau erfolgt, werden im Laufe der Zeit erhebliche Kosten eingespart und die Umwelt geschont. Auch für die Textilien und den Waschvorgang bringt es Vorteile. Denn die automatisch dosierte Menge Waschmittel schont die Wäsche und perfektioniert das Waschergebnis, da eine Über- oder Unterdosierung nahezu ausgeschlossen ist.

Außerdem kommt man nicht mehr bei jedem Waschgang mit dem Waschmittel in Kontakt. Und das Umfeld bleibt wesentlich sauberer.

Die Waschmaschine zeichnet sich durch eine außergewöhnliche Gestaltung aus. Die besondere Akzentuierung im Frontbereich ist ein Alleinstellungsmerkmal. Sie unterliegt dennoch keinen Trends, sondern unterstützt die formale Langlebigkeit wirkungsvoll.

»W 1749 WPS LiquidWash« automatically gauges the liquid detergent, which is stored in a transparent container on the washing machine. It does this with a load-measuring function and a metering pump. All the user has to do is select the desired wash programme and specify how soiled the washing is.

As precisely the right quantity of detergent is added every time, considerable costs are saved in the course of time, and the environment is protected, too. It is also beneficial for the textiles and the washing process. If the quantity of detergent used is automatically correct, washing is gentler on the laundry and produces perfect results, since it is practically impossible to use too much or too little detergent.

Moreover, there is no longer any contact with detergent every time the washing machine is loaded. And this keeps the area around the machine much cleaner.

The washing machine's design is strikingly different. The special accent set by the design of the appliance front is a unique selling point. It is nonetheless not subject to any trends, but effectively underscores its formal longevity.

100

Hausgeräte
Silber

Household appliances
Silver

KM 5997   Kochfeld
Cooking hob

Hersteller / Manufacturer
Miele & Cie. KG
D-33332 Gütersloh

Design / Designer
Werksdesign / In-house design
Andreas Enslin

Vertrieb / Distributor
Miele & Cie. KG
D-33332 Gütersloh

Jury
Überzeugend: Die Idee, die einem Induktionskochfeld zugrunde liegt, ist hier zu Ende gedacht. Einerseits durch übersichtlich angeordnete Kochfelder und die Bedienfreundlichkeit. Andererseits fungiert die Platte, da sie bündig versenkt ist, als erweiterte Arbeitsfläche. Darin liegt auch der Charme dieser Technologie. Und außerdem ist Induktion die derzeit energieärmste Art zu kochen. Die Hitze entsteht nur, wenn der Kochtopf aufgesetzt wird, ist sehr schnell da und kühlt sofort wieder ab. Das ist ökologisch sinnvoll.

Judges panel
Impressive: the basic idea of an induction hob has been taken to its logical conclusion here. On the one hand, in the clear layout of the cooking zones and the hob's user-friendliness. On the other hand, because the hob is flush-mounted, it doubles as an extension of the work surface. This is also what makes this technology so special. What's more, induction is currently the most energy-saving way of cooking. Heat is only generated when the pan is placed on the hob, builds up very quickly and cools down again immediately. This makes ecological sense.

Das Induktionsfeld zeichnet sich durch eine hohe Langlebigkeit und eine großzügige Aufteilung im flächenbündigen Kochfeld aus. Es ist übersichtlich und klar gestaltet und damit sehr bedienerfreundlich – einfach durch ComfortControl Plus-Steuerung.

Die induktive Wärmeübertragung garantiert extrem kurze Ankochzeiten. Die Wärme wird direkt im Topfboden erzeugt. Dadurch erhitzt sich die Glaskeramik geringer. Kochen auf dem Induktionsfeld ist nicht nur komfortabel, sondern spart auch Zeit und Energie, da keine Wärmeverluste entstehen. Durch die automatische Topferkennung, wenn ferromagnetisches Kochgeschirr aufgesetzt wird, wird die Kochzone sehr schnell beheizt. Wird das Kochgeschirr entfernt, stoppt sofort die Energiezufuhr.

Mit einem Timer, der auch als Kurzzeitwecker genutzt werden kann, lässt sich eine Kochdauer von 1-99 Minuten einstellen. Nach Ablauf der vorgegebenen Zeit schaltet die Kochzone automatisch ab.

Designed to be long-lasting, this flush induction hob has generously dimensioned cooking zones. Its elements are clearly arranged and thus very easy to use, with ComfortControl Plus.

Induction heating means that the time taken to heat up food is extremely short. Heat is generated directly in the base of the pan. The ceramic hob itself is heated up less as a result. Cooking on an induction hob is not only convenient, but also saves times and energy, as there is no lost heat. When a ferromagnetic pan is placed on the hob, the automatic pan size recognition function is activated, and the cooking zone heats up rapidly. If the pan is removed, the current is immediately cut off.

A time switch that can also be used as a timer allows cooking times of between 1 and 99 minutes to be set. Once the preset time is up, the cooking zone switches off automatically.

102

Hausgeräte
Silber

Household appliances
Silver

PRS 926 B90E   **Ceran-Gas-Kochstelle**
Ceramic gas hob

Hersteller / Manufacturer
Robert Bosch Hausgeräte GmbH
D-81739 München

Design / Designer
Werksdesign / In-house design
Robert Sachon, Alexander Marsch
Eisele Kuberg Design
Frank Eisele
D-89231 Neu-Ulm

Vertrieb / Distributor
Robert Bosch Hausgeräte GmbH
D-81739 München

Jury
Ein überzeugendes Produkt aus der
Gaskochwelt: Das Design mit Glas sieht
nicht nur schön und zeitgemäß aus, es
vereinfacht auch die Reinigung. Man hat
das Gefühl von einer richtigen Koch-
stelle. Denn wir sollten nicht vergessen:
Kochen ist auch ein Erlebnis. Die Koch-
stelle hat Charakter und sieht sehr schön
aus.

Judges panel
An impressive product from the world of
gas cookers. The glass-based design
not only looks attractive and elegant, but
is also easier to clean. It feels like a real
cooker. After all, we shouldn't forget that
cooking is also an experience. The hob is
distinctive, and is very appealing.

Gerade, wo professionell gekocht wird, sind die
Vorteile von Gas als Primärenergie hochgeschätzt.
Gasflammen zünden sofort und sind nach dem
Ende der Kochzeit sofort aus. Beim Kochen mit Gas
geschieht die Verbrennung direkt dort, wo Wärme gebraucht wird. Deshalb ist der Energieverlust
sehr gering und die Verbrauchskosten niedrig.

Die formvollendete Gas-Glaskeramik-Kochstel-
le »PRS 926 B90E«, die 90 Zentimeter breit ist,
verfügt neben einem großen, zwei Normal- und
einem Sparbrenner über einen Dual-Wokbren-
ner mit hohem Wirkungsgrad und geringem Verbrauch.

Wie es richtiges Kochen mit dem Wok erfordert,
werden mit nur einem Bedienknebel zwei aufein-
ander abgestimmte Flammkreise mit insgesamt
sechs Kilowattstunden aktiviert. Und das bei extrem flacher Bauweise. Das gewährleistet einen
ausgezeichneten Wärmetransfer.

Die gelungene Kombination aller Vorteile von
Gas mit denen der Glaskeramik bietet ein weiteres
Umwelt-Plus durch die leichte Reinigung.

Professional cooks especially appreciate the advantages of gas as a primary energy source. Gas
flames ignite immediately, and are extinguished
as soon as cooking is finished. When cooking
with gas, it is burned directly where the heat is required. Energy loss is therefore minimal, and
running costs low.

The »PRS 926 B90E«, a 90 centimetre-wide, elegant gas ceramic hob, has one large, two standard and one economy burner, plus a highly efficient, economical dual wok burner.

To satisfy the requirements of cooking with a wok,
one control knob ignites two concentric flames
that deliver six kilowatts. This power contrasts with
the extremely flat design, which guarantees excellent transfer of heat.

All the advantages of gas have been well combined with the advantages of ceramic glass, which
provides a further plus for the environment: easy
cleaning.

Öko_Line Geschirrspüler
Dishwasher

Hausgeräte   **Household appliances**
Silber   **Silver**

Öko_Line   **Geschirrspüler**
                 Dishwasher

Hersteller / Manufacturer
Electrolux Major Appliances Europe
B-1830 Zaventem

Design / Designer
AEG Design-Team
D-90429 Nürnberg

Vertrieb / Distributor
Electrolux Vertriebs GmbH
D-90429 Nürnberg

Jury
Einer der bekanntermaßen leisen, energie- und wassersparenden Geschirrspülautomaten von AEG-Electrolux. Uns gefällt, dass er schlicht gestaltet ist und die Bedienelemente gut angeordnet sind. Leicht verständliches Design.

Judges panel
One of the typically quiet, energy-saving and water-saving AEG-Electrolux dishwashers. We liked its unobtrusive design and the way the control elements are arranged. Easily understandable design.

AEG hat bereits vor über 20 Jahren mit der »Öko_Line«-Reihe Pionierarbeit geleistet und setzt seither immer wieder neue Trends mit Geräten, die mehr leisten und dabei weniger Wasser und Energie verbrauchen. Dieser Geschirrspüler ist so ein Gerät.

Er ist äußerst energiesparend. So spült er beispielsweise zwölf Maßgedecke mit nur noch zwölf Litern Wasser und benötigt dafür 1,05 Kilowattstunden. Das ist möglich dank einer innovativen Technologie: Die Beladungserkennung Sensorlogic erkennt die Geschirrmenge und passt automatisch den Wasser- und Stromverbrauch an. So können Energie- und Wasserverbrauch und damit auch die Betriebskosten durchschnittlich um bis zu 20 Prozent verringert werden.

Außerdem ist er extrem leise – nur 44 Dezibel. Sein Design ist durch Schlichtheit und Klarheit geprägt. Das Gerät ist so gestaltet und konstruiert, dass die eingebauten Komponenten, die materialspezifisch gekennzeichnet sind, sich einfach demontieren lassen und gezielt recycelt werden können.

With its »Öko_Line« series, AEG was the pioneer in this area more than 20 years ago. Since then, it has repeatedly set the trend with appliances that are more and more powerful, but at the same time use less energy and water. This dishwasher is just such an appliance.

It consumes very little energy. For example, it can wash twelve standard settings with just twelve litres of water, and consumes just 1.05 kWh. It does so thanks to an innovative technology. Its Sensorlogic load sensor measures the quantity of washing up, and automatically sets the amount of water and electricity needed. In this way, energy and water consumption, and thus operating costs as well, can be reduced by up to 20 percent.

Moreover, the machine is extremely quiet – just 44 decibels. Its design is characterized by unobtrusiveness and clarity. The machine is designed and constructed in such a way that its components, which are labelled to show the materials they are made of, can be easily removed and recycled appropriately.

106

Hausgeräte   Household appliances
Silber   Silver

Classic-Gourmet KSW20 S50   **Stand-Kühlautomat**
Freestanding refrigerator

Hersteller / Manufacturer
Robert Bosch Hausgeräte GmbH
D-81739 München

Design / Designer
Werksdesign / In-house design
Ralph Staud, Thomas Tischer

Vertrieb / Distributor
Robert Bosch Hausgeräte GmbH
D-81739 München

Jury
Hier wurde der Kultkühlschrank von Bosch wieder aufgelegt, aber mit einem zeitgemäßen Innenleben und moderner Technik. Zudem ist er auch energiesparend mit der Energie-Effizienz A+. Sehr schönes Produkt, hochwertige Materialien.

Judges panel
A re-issue of the cult Bosch fridge, but with an up-to-date interior and modern technology. It is also energy-saving, with its A+ rating. Very attractive product, high-quality materials.

Der »Classic-Gourmet KSW20 S50« ist nach dem Vorbild des Bosch-Klassikers, der zum Synonym für den Kühlschrank an sich geworden ist, gestaltet. Was von außen aussieht wie das Kultobjekt aus den 1950er Jahren, ist innen auf dem neuesten Stand der Energiespartechnik.

Bei 184 Liter Nutzinhalt verbraucht der Classic-Gourmet-Kühlschrank nur 122 Kilowattstunden pro Jahr. Er hat die Energie-Effizienz-Klasse A+ und arbeitet auf hohem Stromspar-Niveau.

Der stromlinienförmige, bauchige Kühlschrank mit dem charakteristischen Chromgriff bietet einen schönen Blickfang und seine Innenausstattung zeitgemäßen technologischen Komfort. Neben Abstellflächen aus Glas gibt es einen Flaschenhalter aus Aluminium und eine Ablage aus Holz für Wein- und Sektflaschen. Hochwertige und recycelbare Naturmaterialien, wie Eichenholz und Glas, verbinden Funktionalität mit Design und Umweltschutz.

Ein weiterer Vorteil: Um energietechnisch immer auf dem neuesten Stand der Technik zu bleiben, kann das Innenleben ausgetauscht werden. Denn das selbsttragende Stahlgehäuse ist jederzeit mit einem aktuellen Seriengerät nachrüstbar. Den Stand-Kühlautomaten gibt es in schwarz oder weiß.

»Classic-Gourmet KSW20 S50« is modelled on the Bosch classic that became synonymous with the fridge. What looks like the cult object from the 1950s on the outside offers state-of-the-art energy-saving technology on the inside.

With a net capacity of 184 litres, the Classic Gourmet fridge consumes just 122 kilowatt-hours per year. It is rated as A+ class for energy efficiency, and it is a first-class energy-saver.

The streamlined, slightly bulbous fridge with its characteristic chrome handle is attractive to look at. On the inside, it features the latest technological solutions. Apart from glass shelves, there is an aluminium bottle holder and a wooden shelf for wine and champagne bottles. High-quality recyclable materials such as oak and glass combine functionality with design and environmental protection.

And there is a further plus point. To remain up to date with technological developments, the fridge interior can be replaced. The freestanding steel housing can be refitted at any time with a more current series appliance. The freestanding fridge is available in black or white.

KT 16LP20   Tischkühlschrank
Mini-fridge

Hausgeräte **Household appliances**
Silber **Silver**

KT 16LP20 **Tischkühlschrank**
Mini-fridge

Hersteller / Manufacturer
Siemens-Electrogeräte GmbH
D-81739 München

Design / Designer
Werksdesign / In-house design
Christoph Becke, Max Eicher

Jury
Einfacher kleiner Kühlschrank mit der sehr guten Energie-Effizienz A++. Das kann man lobenswert hervorheben. Siemens hat sich Gedanken gemacht, wie man einen sehr einfachen Kühlschrank hochwertiger gestalten kann. Das ist der erste in dieser Preiskategorie, der eine Glasplatte hat – eine zusätzliche Arbeitsfläche in der Küche. Das ist sehr lobenswert.

Judges panel
Simple, small fridge with an A++ rating. This can be singled out for praise. Siemens has thought about how to improve the quality of a very simple fridge. It is the first one in its category to have a glass top – an additional worktop in the kitchen. This is very commendable.

Der Tischkühlschrank ist mit einer innovativen Besonderheit ausgestattet – einer schnittfesten und hitzeunempfindlichen Arbeitsplatte aus Sicherheitsglas. Die Gestaltung des Gerätes wird durch diese Glasplatte geprägt. Sie garantiert durch ihre Kratzfestigkeit ein hochwertiges Aussehen über den gesamten Lebenszyklus des Kühlschranks. Diese Besonderheit hebt das Gerät aus der Masse des niedrigpreisigen Kostensegments heraus.

Durch die hochwertige Technik erreicht das Kühlgerät die Energie-Effizienz-Klasse A++. Die Materialien lassen sich leicht trennen und recyceln.

Er kann auch mit einem Gefrierschrank aus dieser Gerätereihe zu einem hocheffizienten und preisgünstigen Geräte-Set kombiniert werden.

This mini-fridge is equipped with an innovative special feature, a scratch-resistant and heatproof worktop made of safety glass. The appliance's design is determined by this glass top. Because it is scratch-resistant, it guarantees that the fridge will have the same high-quality appearance throughout its service life. This special feature sets the appliance apart from the broad mass in the low-price segment.

Thanks to outstanding technology, the fridge is rated A++ for energy efficiency. Its materials can be easily separated and recycled.

It can also be combined with a freezer from the same series to form a highly efficient and inexpensive set.

Focus in Gold

Küche   **Kitchens**
Gold   **Gold**

Eva Solo   **Reibeimer**
             Grating bucket

Hersteller / Manufacturer
Eva Denmark A/S
DK-2760 Måløv

Design / Designer
Tools Design®
Claus Jensen & Henrik Holbæk
DK-2400 Kopenhagen NV

Vertrieb / Distributor
Eva Denmark A/S
DK-2760 Måløv

Wunderbares Beispiel für ein Kombi-Tool, wo man mehrere Dinge, die man in der Küche für eine Tätigkeit braucht, zusammengelegt hat. Der Designer, der das gemacht hat, hat sehr gut geschaut, betrachtet und analysiert. Und hat dann eine sehr schlaue, sehr einfache Lösung gefunden. Das ist Design, das besser nicht sein kann.

Wonderful example of a tool that combines several things that are needed when working in the kitchen. The designer who made this did a very good job of observing, considering and analyzing. And when he had finished, he came up with a very clever, very simple solution. Design doesn't come any better than this.

Der Reibeimer stellt die herkömmliche Reibe auf den Kopf und schafft eine völlig neue Funktionalität: Er vereint zwei Produkte in einem. Werden Karotten, Gurken und Äpfel geraspelt oder Käse gerieben, fängt der Eimer das Reibgut – und selbst überschüssige Flüssigkeit – auf. Zudem lässt sich anschließend der Inhalt viel bequemer in Schüsseln und Töpfe umschütten.

Der Reibeimer ersetzt die bei herkömmlichen Reiben notwendigen Schüsseln oder Teller. Somit muss nur der Reibeimer gespült werden, – ein ökologischer Fortschritt. Der Reibeimer ist aus Edelstahl und spülmaschinenfest.

This grating bucket turns the conventional grater on its head, creating a completely new function. It combines two products in one. If carrots, cucumbers, apples or cheese are grated, the grated food, and any surplus liquid, falls into the bucket. Moreover, it is then much easier to transfer the contents to a bowl or saucepan.

The grating bucket replaces the bowls or plates that are needed with conventional graters. As a result, only the grating bucket has to be washed up – an ecological plus. The grating bucket is made of stainless steel, and is dishwasher-safe.

114

Küche   Kitchens
Silber   Silver

**Balance   Küchenwaage
Kitchen scales**

Hersteller / Manufacturer
Maywerk Gmbh
D-42115 Wuppertal

Design / Designer
Werksdesign / In-house design

Vertrieb / Distributor
Maywerk Gmbh
D-42115 Wuppertal

»Balance« verbindet eine traditionelle Arbeits- und Funktionsweise mit modernem Design. Die Küchenwaage basiert auf dem bewährten und präzisen Prinzip der Balkenwaage. Diese Waagenbauart ist rein mechanisch – sie funktioniert ganz ohne komplizierte Elektronik und Batterie – und kommt mit wenigen Bauteilen aus. Zum Wiegen wird das gewünschte Gewicht bis zu zwei Kilogramm voreingestellt, indem das Laufgewicht auf der Wippe verschoben wird. Man füllt dann beispielsweise Mehl oder Reis ein, bis die Waage im Gleichgewicht und das gewählte Gewicht erreicht ist. Das erkennt man, wie bei einer Wasserwaage, an einer Luftblase in einer markierten Feinanzeige.

»Balance« zeichnet sich auch durch seine hochwertigen Materialien aus: für den sehr festen Waagenkörper technisches Aluminium, das in verschiedenen Farben mit einer sehr harten Eloxalschicht veredelt wird, für die Gefäße Thüringer Hartporzellan und für das Kunststofflager, auf dem das Laufgewicht gleitet, POM.

Alle Komponenten der funktionalen und langlebigen Küchenwaage werden von umweltzertifizierten Zulieferern innerhalb Deutschlands und Österrreichs bezogen.

»Balance« combines a traditional method and function with modern design. The kitchen scales are based on the tried and tested, precise principle of the beam balance. The scales are purely mechanical in design. They work without any complicated electronics or batteries, and are made up of just a few components. To weigh food, the desired weight (up to two kilograms) is preset by sliding the weight along the beam. Then the food – flour or rice, for example – is poured in until the scales balance and the selected weight is reached. This is shown by an air bubble in a calibrated scale, similar to a spirit level.

»Balance« is also remarkable for its high-quality materials: industrial aluminium treated with a very hard anodized coating in various colours for the high-tensile body of the scales, Thuringian hard porcelain for the pans, and polyoxymethylene (POM) for the plastic bearing along which the sliding weight moves.

All the components of these functional, long-lasting kitchen scales are procured from environmentally certified suppliers in Germany and Austria.

Küche   Kitchens
Silber   Silver

Time Savers »Speedy Chef«   **Küchenhilfe**
Kitchen aid

Hersteller / Manufacturer
Tupperware Belgium N.V.
B-9300 Aalst

Design / Designer
Werksdesign / In-house design
Vincent Jalet

Vertrieb / Distributor
Tupperware Deutschland GmbH
D-60488 Frankfurt a. M.

Jury
Sehr schönes Beispiel eines mit Muskelkraft betriebenen Produktes. Es ersetzt elektrische Rührgeräte und spart so natürlich sehr viel Energie. Gleichzeitig ist es vom Design her so motivierend gestaltet, dass man richtig Lust hat, es zu benutzen. Durch die Anordnung der Rührquirle, die ein bisschen versetzt angeordnet sind, wird die effiziente Übertragung der Muskelkraft aufs Rührgut noch mal verstärkt. Sehr gut gestaltet.

Judges panel
Very nice example of a product driven by muscle power. It is an alternative to electrical mixers, which of course means it saves a lot of energy. At the same time, its design is so motivating that you really want to try it out. The way the whisks have been arranged slightly out of line amplifies the efficient transmission of muscle power to the mixture in the jug. Excellently designed.

Ohne Elektrizität kann man mit »Speedy Chef« nicht nur Eiweiß, Sahne, Omelette und Mayonnaise schlagen, sondern auch alle Sorten von Dessertcremes, Teig und Dressings rühren. Dabei ist der Küchenhelfer schneller und leiser als ein elektrisches Rührgerät – beispielsweise lassen sich mit ihm drei Eiweiß in 25 Sekunden schlagen. Er ist sehr leicht zu bedienen für Linkshänder ebenso wie für Rechtshänder.

Der manuell betriebene Küchenhelfer besteht aus zwei getrennten Teilen: dem Messbecher und dem Deckel mit integriertem Griff, Dichtungsring, oberer Abdeckung und Rührbesen. Alle Teile lassen sich schnell und bequem zusammenbauen und zum Reinigen zerlegen.

Der Messbecher fasst einen Liter. Seine Durchsichtigkeit erlaubt, den Inhalt während des Schlagens oder Rührens gut zu beobachten und zu überwachen. Im Griff ist ein Trichter integriert, um beispielsweise Öl oder Gewürze, ohne den Deckel zu öffnen, zuzugeben. Nach dem Rühren kann die Speise einfach im Messbecher – mit einem Deckel – in den Kühlschrank zum Kühlen gestellt werden. »Speedy Chef« ist sehr ergonomisch und bedienerfreundlich gestaltet: die eine Hand kann leicht den Deckel halten während die andere mühelos den Griff dreht.

The »Speedy Chef« can be used not only to whip egg whites, cream, omelettes and mayonnaise, but also to mix all kinds of creamy desserts, pastry and dressings – and this without electricity. The kitchen aid is also faster and quieter than an electric mixer. For example, 3 egg whites can be beaten in 25 seconds. It is easy to use, both for left and right-handers.

The manually operated kitchen aid is made of two separate parts: the measuring jug and the lid. The latter comes with an integrated handle, seal, top cover and whisk. All the parts can be assembled quickly and easily, and taken apart again for cleaning.

The measuring jug holds one liter. Because it is transparent, an eye can be kept on the contents when whipping or mixing. The handle has a funnel integrated into its base, which allows oil or spices to be added without opening the lid. After mixing, the food can be left in the measuring jug and kept cool in the refrigerator. »Speedy Chef« is very ergonomic and user-friendly in design: one hand can easily hold the lid while the other effortlessly turns the handle.

Full Contact™   Mikrowellen- und Tiefkühl-Behälter
Microwave and deep-freeze container

Küche   **Kitchens**
Silber   **Silver**

Full Contact™   **Mikrowellen- und Tiefkühl-Behälter**
Microwave and deep-freeze container

Hersteller / Manufacturer
Tupperware France S.A.
F-37300 Joué-lès-Tours

Design / Designer
Jan-Hendrik de Groote, Dimitri Backaert
Tupperware Belgium N.V.
B-9300 Aalst

Vertrieb / Distributor
Tupperware Deutschland GmbH
D-60488 Frankfurt a. M.

Ein Produkt – zwei Funktionen. »Full Contact™« ist Gefrier- und Mikrowellenbehälter in einem. Der Behälter ist so gestaltet, dass er Nahrungsmittel viel schneller und schonender als andere Behälter einfriert.

So passt sich der flexible weiche Deckel aus Silikon dem Inhalt an, damit beim Einfrieren möglichst wenig Luft im Behälter bleibt. Das verhindert Gefrierbrand, die Lebensmittel werden bis zu 30 Prozent schneller eingefroren und Vitamine und Mineralstoffe bleiben so bestmöglich erhalten. Auch die vier hervorgehobenen Ecken begünstigen das schnellere Einfrieren, weil dadurch die kalte Luft besser um den Behälter zirkulieren kann. Die Behälter sind temperaturbeständig von minus 25°C bis plus 160°C, sodass sie direkt vom Gefrierschrank in die Mikrowelle zum Auftauen und Erwärmen gestellt werden können.

Es gibt die Behälter in zwei Größen. Der 1,3-Liter-Behälter bietet sich für großvolumige Speisen an wie etwa für einen Braten, Brot, Fenchelknollen oder Broccoli. Der zweite Behälter fasst 800 Milliliter und eignet sich zum Beispiel mehr für längliches Gemüse, wie Maiskolben oder Lauchstangen oder für weniger voluminöses Fleisch wie Steaks und Gulasch.

One product – two functions. »Full Contact™« is a container for both the freezer and the microwave. It is designed in such a way that food is frozen faster and more gently than in other containers.

The flexible soft silicon lid takes on the form of the contents, with the result that as little air as possible remains in the container on freezing. This prevents freezer burn, the food freezes up to 30 percent faster, and vitamins and minerals are conserved as efficiently as possible. The four raised corners also help the food to freeze faster, because they allow the cold air to circulate better around the container. The containers can withstand temperatures from -25°C to 160°C, which means that they can be taken straight from the freezer to the microwave for thawing and heating.

The containers are available in two sizes. The 1.3 litre container is suitable for bulky foods such as a joint of meat, a loaf of bread, fennel bulbs or broccoli. The second container has a capacity of 800 millilitres, and is more suitable for long vegetables such as maize or leeks, or for less bulky meat such as steaks or stewing meat.

120

Küche Kitchens
Silber Silver

Fine Bone China **Teller, Platten, Schüsseln**
Plates, platters, bowls

Hersteller / Manufacturer
B.T. Dibbern GmbH & Co. KG
D-22941 Bargteheide

Design / Designer
Werksdesign / In-house design
Dibbern Design Studio

Vertrieb / Distributor
B.T. Dibbern GmbH & Co. KG
D-22941 Bargteheide

Jury
Ganz schlicht und klassisch gestaltete Porzellanserie, die aus feinem Bone China besteht und in Deutschland gefertigt wird mit minimalem Materialeinsatz und mit wirklich dünnen und filigranen Wandstärken. Man kann im Grunde genommen heute schon den Designklassiker voraussagen. Langlebiges Design.

Judges panel
Very tasteful, classically designed series made of fine bone china. Made in Germany with a minimum of materials, the end product is very thin and filigree. Basically, we can predict this will be a design classic. Designed to be long-lasting.

Die Teller werden noch nach traditioneller Art von Hand gedreht und nicht, wie in der industriellen Massenfertigung, gepresst. Dadurch wird eine besonders dünne Scherbenstärke mit einer unerreicht hohen Stabilität und damit hohem Gebrauchswert erzeugt. Die Feinheit und Dichte des Scherbens und der warme Farbton entstehen dadurch, dass Knochenasche beigemischt wird.

Fine Bone China ist die technisch und handwerklich anspruchsvollste Stufe der keramischen Fertigung. Die hoch widerstandsfähige Porzellanserie ist sehr schlicht, zurückhaltend und zeitlos gestaltet. Auffallend ist auch die große Flachheit und die Transparenz mit einem zarten Schimmer.

Es werden nur bleifreie Glasuren verwendet, und produziert wird das Porzellan ausschließlich im eigenen Werk in Deutschland.

These plates are still made the traditional way, being turned by hand and not pressed as is usual in industrial mass production. The result is a very thin body that is exceptionally robust and has a high utility value. The thinness and density of the body, as well as its warm colour, are the result of mixing in bone ash.

Technically and in terms of craftsmanship, Fine Bone China is the most sophisticated form of ceramic production. This series of very tough porcelain is very unostentatious and timeless in design. A further remarkable feature is its extreme flatness and its transparency, with a delicate sheen.

Only lead-free glaze is used, and the porcelain is produced exclusively in the company's own plant in Germany.

122

Küche **Kitchens**
Silber **Silver**

Quooker® PRO3-VAQ **Kochendwasserhahn**
Tap for boiling water

Hersteller / Manufacturer
Quooker®
Peteri B.V.
NL-2984 AJ Ridderkerk

Design / Designer
Werksdesign / In-house design

Vertrieb / Distributor
Quooker Deutschland GmbH
Marc Brinker
D-40217 Düsseldorf

Jury
Eine Alternative zum Wasserkocher
und zur Kaffee- oder Teemaschine. Man
kann das Wasser dosieren, wie man es
tatsächlich benötigt. Und das Gerät verbraucht ganz wenig Strom, weil das
Heißwasser-Reservoir gut isoliert ist.
Zusätzlich zur Verfügbarkeit von ko-
chend heißem Wasser reinigt das Gerät
das Wasser auch. Es filtert Kalk. Dadurch schmecken Tee und Kaffee besser.

Judges panel
An alternative to the kettle, as well as to
the coffee or tea-maker. You take as
much water as you actually need. And the
appliance consumes very little electricity because the hot-water tank is well
insulated. Apart from supplying boiling
hot water, the appliance also cleans
the water. It filters calcium bicarbonate
out of the water. As a result, limescale
does not build up so often, and tea and
coffee taste better.

Der »Quooker« liefert kochendes Wasser aus
dem Wasserhahn beispielsweise für Tee, Kaffee
und Spaghettiwasser oder auch um Marmela-
dengläser auszuspülen und Tomaten zu schälen.

Das System besteht aus einer Armatur und einem
kleinen Reservoir für drei Liter Wasser, das an
die Wasserleitung und den Kochendwasserhahn
angeschlossen ist. Das Wasser im Reservoir
wird elektrisch auf 110°C erhitzt und auf dieser
Temperatur gehalten. Wird kochendes Wasser
entnommen, strömt gleichzeitig kaltes Wasser
nach, das automatisch erwärmt wird.

»Quooker« schont die Ressourcen, da er ener-
gie- und wassersparend ist. Durch seine patentierte Hochvakuumisolierung hält das Reservoir
kochendes Wasser jederzeit bereit. Strom wird nur
für das Erhitzen des entnommenen Wassers verbraucht, und das sind weniger als 10 Watt pro Tag.
Zudem wird im Gegensatz zu den üblichen Wasserkochern, wo man häufig zu viel Wasser erhitzt,
nur die tatsächlich benötigte Wassermenge verbraucht.

Bevor das Wasser das Reservoir verlässt, wird es
zudem durch einen Filter gereinigt, entkeimt
und entkalkt. Das erhöht die Qualität des Wassers
gegenüber dem aus üblichen Wasserkochern.
Der Druck-Dreh-Knopf schützt Kinder vor unbe-
absichtigtem Öffnen des Hahns.

The »Quooker« supplies boiling water from the
tap, for tea or coffee for example, for cooking spa-
ghetti, for rinsing out jam jars, or for peeling to-
matoes.

The system comprises a tap and a small tank
for three litres of water, which is connected to the
mains water supply and the boiling water tap.
The water in the tank is heated electrically to 110°C
and kept at this temperature. If boiling water is
drawn off, cold water flows into the tank and is
automatically heated.

»Quooker« conserves resources, since it saves
both energy and water. The tank's patented high-
vacuum insulation means that boiling water is
always available. Electricity is only used to heat
the water drawn off, which means it consumes
less than 10 watts per day. And unlike conventional kettles, where too much water is frequently
heated, only the water that is actually needed
is consumed.

Before the water leaves the tank, moreover, it is
cleaned, sterilized and decalcified. This means the
water is of a higher quality than water from conventional kettles. The push-and-turn handle means
that children cannot accidentally turn the tap.

Interior   Interiors
Gold   Gold

Emeco 20-06 Chair   Stapelstuhl
Stackable chair

Hersteller / Manufacturer
Emeco
Hanover, PA 17331
USA

Design / Designer
Foster + Partners Ltd.
GB-London SW11 4AN

Vertrieb / Distributor
Möbelagentur Goeschen
D-91058 Erlangen

Jury
Ein Designklassiker, neu aufgelegt mit weniger Materialverbrauch und aus Recyclingmaterial – wunderbar. Ein schönes Beispiel, weil die Wandstärken hier wirklich auf ein Minimum reduziert wurden und das Material – Aluminium – Leichtigkeit vermittelt. Sehr hochwertig verarbeitet und die Schweißnähte überall sauber verputzt: ein schönes Objekt.

Judges panel
A re-issue of a design classic, using less material and recycled materials – wonderful. A good example, because the thickness of the walls has truly been reduced to a minimum here, and the material used – aluminium – conveys a feeling of lightness. Very high-quality workmanship, all the welds have been ground smooth: a beautiful object.

In dem Stuhl verbinden sich fortschrittliche Technologie, originelle Geometrie, moderne Form, Liebe zum Detail und Sensibilität für ökologische Erfordernisse mit hoher Handwerkskunst. Der »Emeco 20-06« besteht aus recyceltem Aluminium, 80 Prozent davon stammt aus einer Mischung von Konsum- und Industrieabfall.

Obwohl er extrem leicht ist, zeichnet er sich durch hohe Stabilität aus. Dank seiner schlichten, zeitlosen Form mit der ökonomischen, nahtlosen Silhouette ist er langlebig. Vorbild war der Navy® Chair, der für U-Boote im Zweiten Weltkrieg gemacht wurde. Der »Emeco 20-06« verkörpert die Essenz des Navy® Chair jedoch mit einer veredelten Struktur und einer modernen Anmutung.

Der ultradünne Rahmen besteht aus gehärtetem Aluminium. Der ergonomisch geformte Sitz und Rücken sind handgeschweißt. Obwohl der leichtgewichtige Stuhl enorm stabil ist, braucht er 15 Prozent weniger Aluminium als der Original Navy® Chair.

»Emeco 20-06« hat 40 Jahre Garantie und wie das Vorbild eine geschätzte 150-jährige Lebensdauer. Zehn Stühle lassen sich bequem übereinander stapeln.

This chair combines advanced technology, original geometry, modern form, an eye for detail and sensitivity for ecological requirements with outstanding artisanal skill. The »Emeco 20-06« is made of recycled aluminium, 80 percent of which is a mixture of post-consumer and post-industrial waste.

Although extremely light, it is very sturdy. Thanks to its unassuming, timeless form with its economical, seamless silhouette, it is long-lasting. It was modelled on the Navy® chair, which was made for submarines in the second world war. »Emeco 20-06« embodies the essence of the Navy® Chair, but it has been given a more refined structure and modern air.

The ultra-thin frame is made of hardened aluminium. The ergonomically shaped seat and back are hand-welded. Although the lightweight chair is extremely sturdy, 15 percent less aluminium is used to make it than the original Navy® chair.

»Emeco 20-06« comes with a 40-year guarantee, and an estimated service life of 150 years, just like the chair on which it was modelled. Ten chairs can easily be stacked on top of each other.

Andoo Lounge Chair   Sessel
Easy chair

Interior **Interiors**
Silber **Silver**

Andoo Lounge Chair   **Sessel**
Easy chair

Hersteller / Manufacturer
Walter Knoll AG & Co. KG
D-71083 Herrenberg

Design / Designer
EOOS Design GmbH
A-1010 Wien

Vertrieb / Distributor
Walter Knoll AG & Co. KG
D-71083 Herrenberg

Jury
Der Lounge-Chair ist unglaublich zeitlos. Den könnte man schon 1905 gesehen haben, aber auch 2055 noch sehen. Und das ist das Schöne an dem Sessel. Extrem hochwertig verarbeitet, hervorragende Materialität, sehr schöne Details, handwerklich wunderbar gemacht. Das ist ein Sessel, den man über Generationen vererben kann. Schon aus diesem Grund ein ökologisches Produkt.

Judges panel
The lounge chair is incredibly timeless. You could have seen a chair like this in 1905, or still see one like it in 2055. And that is what is so attractive about this easy chair. Very high-quality workmanship, excellent materials, very appealing details, a wonderful piece of craftsmanship. This is a chair that can be handed down as an heirloom. For this reason alone, an ecological product.

»Andoo« besticht auf den ersten Blick durch seine Einfachheit. Erst auf den zweiten Blick erschließt sich seine Komplexität: exzellente handwerkliche Verarbeitung, raffinierte Einzüge in den weichen Kissen, aufwändige Keder-Steppungen – die Verstärkung von Kanten und Nähten –, die die Lederflächen gliedern, eine Lederauflage, die das Sitzkissen vom Holzrahmen trennt. Holzarmlehnen, die wirken als wären sie gegossen.

Bei dem Sessel mit der minimalistischen Formensprache werden nur hochwertige, natürliche Materialien aus nachwachsenden Rohstoffen verarbeitet. Das Gestell ist aus Massivholz, Nussbaum, Buche oder Eiche. Der Bezug in Reinanillin-Leder gewährleistet eine angenehme, natürliche Haptik und fast unbegrenzte Haltbarkeit. Nicht nur das, sondern auch das zurückhaltende Design macht den Sessel zu einem zeitlosen Klassiker und nachhaltigen Produkt.

»Andoo« gibt es in verschiedenen Varianten: mit hohem und niederem Rücken, mit und ohne Armlehnen oder auch mit Polstersitz.

The first impression »Andoo« makes is one of simplicity. It is only a second look that reveals its complexity: excellent craftsmanship, sophisticated tufting in the soft upholstery, extravagant piping – reinforcing edges and seams – that divides up the leather surfaces, a leather cover that separates the upholstery from the wooden frame, and wooden arm rests that appear to have been moulded.

For this easy chair with its minimalist formal expression, only high-quality, natural materials from renewable resources have been used. The frame is made of solid walnut, beech or oak. The upholstery of pure aniline leather guarantees a pleasant, natural feeling and almost unlimited durability. Combined with its unassuming design, this makes the easy chair a timeless design classic, as well as a sustainable product.

»Andoo« is available in various models: with a high or low back, with or without armrests, or with an upholstered seat.

Mosspink Sofa
          Sofa

Interior   Interiors
Silber   Silver

Mosspink   **Sofa**
           Sofa

           Hersteller / Manufacturer
           Brühl
           D-95138 Bad Steben-Carlsgrün

           Design / Designer
           Kati Meyer-Brühl
           D-95138 Bad Steben-Carlsgrün

           Vertrieb / Distributor
           Brühl
           D-95138 Bad Steben-Carlsgrün

Jury
Das Sofa zeichnet sich durch hervorragende Materialwahl aus. Es ist nach nachhaltigen Prinzipien hergestellt, die Firma arbeitet sehr gut und hat hohe Standards sowohl was Mitarbeiter als auch Materialverarbeitung und Qualität anbelangt. Alle Stoffbezüge oder Lederbezüge sind nach nachhaltigen Kriterien ausgewählt. Sehr überzeugend. Schön ist die sehr modulare und flexible Gestaltung. Man kann das Sofa puristisch als Fläche nutzen oder verschiedene Elemente aufstecken.

Judges panel
The sofa stands out by virtue of the excellent materials chosen. It is manufactured according to sustainable principles, the company works very well and to high standards, both in relation to its employees and to the processing of materials and quality. All the fabric and leather covers have been selected according to the criteria of sustainability. Very impressive. The very modular, flexible design is appealing. The sofa can be used purely as a seating surface, or different elements can be added on.

»Mosspink« ist von der Natur inspiriert, organische Formen schichten sich übereinander. Das Sofa ist aus wenigen Komponenten aufgebaut: einem soliden Holzuntergestell, einer hochwertigen Polsterauflage und drei verschiedenen Polsterlehnen. Diese drei Lehnen in originellen Formen – organisch rund oder schräg – und verschiedenen Farben lassen sich spielerisch mit der homogenen Sofabasis kombinieren.

Alle Herstellungswege sind ökologisch ausgerichtet: von den beständigen, schadstoffarmen Materialien bis hin zur Wiederverwertung von Restmaterialien. So sind die Bezüge von »Mosspink« entweder aus natürlichen, umweltfreundlichen Stoffen oder aus hochwertigem Leder, dessen Zuschnittreste zu Schuhen, Handschuhen und Geldbeuteln weiterverarbeitet werden.

Bei Brühl wird Nachhaltigkeit und Verantwortung aber noch sehr viel weiter gefasst. So wird der Einsatz von gesundheitlich bedenklichen Stoffen permanent reduziert und wo möglich ersetzt. Beispielsweise wurden die Schadstoffwerte, denen die Mitarbeiter in den Spritzkabinen der Klebe-Anlage ausgesetzt sind, auf weniger als ein Prozent vom gesetzlichen Grenzwert gesenkt und sind damit kaum noch nachweisbar. Zudem wird auch bei den Mitarbeitern hohe Eigenverantwortung gefördert und gefordert, was sich in den ganzheitlichen Arbeitsgängen und letztendlich der hohen Verarbeitungsqualität widerspiegelt.

»Mosspink« is inspired by nature. Organic forms are layered on top of each other. The sofa is made up of just a few components: A robust wooden frame, a high-quality upholstered base and three different upholstered rest elements. These three rest elements come in original shapes – organically round or asymmetrical – and different colours, and can be combined playfully with the homogeneous sofa base.

All the manufacturing processes are guided by ecological concerns: from the long-lasting, low-polluting materials to the recycling of leftover materials. The covers of »Mosspink«, for example, are either made of natural, environmentally friendly fabrics or of high-quality leather, the leftovers of which are processed to make shoes, gloves and purses.

At Brühl, however, sustainability and responsibility mean far more than this. For example, the use of substances that present a health hazard is permanently reduced, and alternatives are found wherever possible. The hazardous materials to which employees are exposed when spraying adhesives have been reduced to less than one percent of the legal limit, and are therefore barely detectable. In addition, employees are expected and encouraged to take on responsibility for their work, and this is reflected in integrated work processes and, in the end, a high quality of workmanship.

Interior   Interiors
Silber   Silver

Siebenschläfer   **Bett**
Bed

Hersteller / Manufacturer
Nils Holger Moormann GmbH
D-83229 Aschau i. Chiemgau

Design / Designer
Christoffer Martens/erstererster
D-10437 Berlin

Vertrieb / Distributor
Nils Holger Moormann GmbH
D-83229 Aschau i. Chiemgau

Jury

Das Interessante an diesem Bettentwurf ist, dass es eine komplette Stecklösung ist und keinerlei Metallteile enthält. Die Idee ist gut, dass man mit L-förmigen Elementen arbeitet, die spiegelverkehrt aus einem quadratischen oder rechteckigen Stück Holz herausgesägt werden können. Holz ist ein nachwachsender Rohstoff, materialeffizient und stabil. Reduziertes Design, klassisch, schlicht und langlebig.

Judges panel

What is interesting about this bed design is that it is assembled solely by slotting pieces into place, and contains absolutely no metal parts. A good idea to work with L-shaped elements that can be sawn out of a square or rectangular piece of wood, with one element mirroring the other. Wood is a renewable resource. This makes efficient use of the materials, and it is robust. Reduced design, classic, unassuming and long-lasting.

»Siebenschläfer« besticht durch seine minimalistische, zeitlose Gestaltung. Der Rahmen besteht aus Furniersperrholz – Birke – in den Farben weiß, schwarz oder rot und der Lattenrost aus unbehandelter Esche. Das Bett gibt es mit Kopfteil und ohne.

Das Bett ist völlig metallfrei konstruiert und aus nachwachsenden Rohstoffen regional gefertigt. Dadurch sind die Transportwege auf ein Minimum reduziert. Zusätzlich erhöhen niedrige Energiekosten bei der Verarbeitung die Umweltfreundlichkeit des Bettes.

In Einzelteilen lässt es sich für einen problemlosen Transport auf ein geringes Packmaß reduzieren. Zum Aufbau lassen sich die Einzelteile von »Siebenschläfer« einfach ohne Werkzeug zusammenstecken.

»Siebenschläfer's« design is strikingly minimalist and timeless. The frame is made of birch veneer plywood stained white, black or red, and the slats of untreated ash. The bed is available with or without a headboard.

It is made completely without metal, and manufactured locally using renewable materials. This means that transport is reduced to a minimum. And what makes the bed even more environmentally friendly is the low amount of energy consumed when constructing it.

As it can be knocked down to a small package, transporting it is no problem. And to put it back together again, »Siebenschläfer's« parts are easy to assemble, with no need for tools.

134

Abgemahnt   **Beistelltisch**
Side table

Hersteller / Manufacturer
Nils Holger Moormann GmbH
D-83229 Aschau i. Chiemgau

Design / Designer
Werksdesign / In-house design

Vertrieb / Distributor
Nils Holger Moormann GmbH
D-83229 Aschau i. Chiemgau

Jury
Ein schlichtes Produkt, das lustig und ganz einfach für die Produktion ist. Der Tisch macht Spaß. Ein emotionales Produkt mit Persönlichkeit.

Judges panel
An unassuming product that is fun, and very simple to produce. An amusing table. An emotional product with personality.

Der kleine Beistelltisch lässt sich ganz schnell und bequem überall hin stellen, wo man ihn gerade haben möchte. Diese Mobilität erhält er durch einen Bügel, der die Tischplatte asymmetrisch durchdringt und als Griff dient.

Er zeichnet sich durch seine minimalistische und puristische Gestaltung aus. Er besteht lediglich aus einem massiven Fichtenholzfuß, einem warmgewalzten und gewachsten Stahlgestell und einer Furniersperrholz-Tischplatte aus Birke in den Farben weiß, schwarz oder rot.

Der Tisch wird mit niedrigen Energiekosten und aus überwiegend nachwachsenden Rohstoffen in der Region gefertigt, wodurch nur geringe Transportwege entstehen.

This small side table can be quickly and conveniently placed wherever it is needed. It is so easy to move thanks to a hoop that divides the table asymmetrically, and serves as a handle.

Its design is strikingly minimalist and purist. All it comprises are a base of solid spruce, a hot-rolled and waxed steel frame and a birch veneer plywood table top, available in white, black or red.

Little energy is consumed when manufacturing the table, which is made locally with mainly renewable materials, which in turn keeps transport to a minimum.

Bellocha Tisch
Table

Interior **Interiors**
Silber **Silver**

Bellocha **Tisch**
Table

Hersteller / Manufacturer
Constantine Furniture
D-74547 Kupfer

Design / Designer
Werksdesign / In-house design

Vertrieb / Distributor
Constantine Furniture
D-74547 Kupfer

Jury
Der Tisch ist handwerklich sehr schön gemacht. Die Gestaltung mit den Beinen, die praktisch die Tischplatte durchdringen, ist überzeugend umgesetzt. Ein dynamisches Element, das die klassische Form durchbricht. Es ist einfach schön, einen reinen sauberen Holztisch zu sehen, der aber keine altmodische Anmutung hat.

Judges panel
The table is beautifully crafted. The way it is designed, with legs that practically penetrate the table top, has been impressively executed. A dynamic element that transfixes its classic form. It is good to see a pure, unadorned wooden table that does not create an old-fashioned impression.

Der Tisch erhält durch seine abgeschrägte Tischplatte eine Leichtigkeit, die für seine Größe außergewöhnlich ist. Ein besonderes Gestaltungsmerkmal sind die abgewinkelten und formschönen Beine, die dem Tisch eine ganz eigene Formensprache und eine emotionale Identität geben.

Es werden nur einheimische Hölzer aus nachhaltiger Forstwirtschaft verwendet. Gefertigt wird er in Handarbeit und ausschließlich in Deutschland. Die Oberflächen sind nur mit ökologischem Wachs behandelt.

Man kann den Tisch in verschiedenen Ausführungen und unterschiedlichen Holztönen erhalten.

The bevelled table top gives this table a lightness that is unusual for his size. Its angled, elegant legs are a special design feature, giving the table a formal expression and an emotional identity all of its own.

Only locally grown timber from sustainable forestry is used. It is hand-crafted exclusively in Germany. The surfaces are treated solely with ecological wax.

The table is available in various designs and in different wood types.

Focus in Gold

Think   Arbeitsstuhl
Office chair

140

Objektmöblierung
Gold

Contract furniture
Gold

Think   **Arbeitsstuhl**
Office chair

Hersteller / Manufacturer
Steelcase Werndl AG
D-83026 Rosenheim

Design / Designer
Glen Oliver Löw
Industrial Design
D-20249 Hamburg

Vertrieb / Distributor
Steelcase Werndl AG
D-83026 Rosenheim

Jury
Ein gut gestalteter Bürostuhl, der das Prinzip »von der Wiege bis zur Bahre« konsequent verfolgt. Er ist komplett zerleg- und recycelbar. Oberflächenbeschichtungen sind vermieden worden und das Aluminium wird nur poliert. Man produziert in Kundennähe, was die Transportwege verkürzt. Ein umfassend ökologisches Produkt.

Judges panel
A well designed office chair that consistently adheres to the »from the cradle to the grave« principle. It can be completely knocked down, and all its parts are recyclable. The surfaces have not been treated. Instead, the aluminium has just been polished. The chair is produced near to where the customers are, which keeps transport distances down. A thoroughly ecological product.

Bei der Entwicklung von »Think« wurden die Umweltauswirkungen aller Phasen des Produkt-Lebenszyklus – von der Rohstoffgewinnung über Produktion, Transport und Nutzung bis hin zu Recycling und Entsorgung – mit Hilfe einer Lebenszyklus-Analyse (LCA-ISO 14044) ermittelt und reduziert. Auf diese Weise konnte ein wirklich nachhaltiges Produkt entworfen werden.

So wird er nicht nur zu 44 Prozent aus recycelten Materialien hergestellt, sondern lässt sich nach seinem Produktleben extrem einfach in nur fünf Minuten in seine Komponenten zerlegen, die wiederum zu 99 Prozent zu verwerten sind. Um den Transportaufwand zu reduzieren, werden die Stühle jeweils in der Nähe der Kunden in Europa, Asien und Nordamerika produziert. Es wurden nur Materialien verwendet, die als umweltsicher gelten. Der Stuhl wurde so designt, dass Abfälle, Energieverbrauch und Umweltauswirkungen möglichst gering sind. Damit ist »Think«, für den eine Umweltprodukterklärung (EPD = Environmental Product Declaration) erstellt wurde, über seinen gesamten Lebenszyklus hinweg ein umweltschonender Stuhl.

»Think« denkt aber auch mit. So passt er sich intuitiv an den Körper und die Körperbewegungen an. Seine Rückenlehne gibt Halt entsprechend dem Körpergewicht und dem bevorzugten Arbeitsstil des Nutzers. Er verfügt über einfache Bedienelemente. »Mein Komfort™ control« bietet beispielsweise vier Möglichkeiten, den Schwingungsgrad der Rückenlehne einzustellen.

When developing »Think«, a life-cycle analysis (LCA-ISO 14044) was done to calculate and reduce the environmental impact of every phase of the product life-cycle – from extraction and production of raw materials, via production, transport and use, to recycling and disposal. This allowed a truly sustainable product to be designed.

It is not only made of materials that are 44 percent recycled, but at the end of its useful life it can also be broken down extremely easily into its component materials, which themselves can then be 99 percent recycled. To keep transport to a minimum, the chairs are produced in the proximity of their customers, in Europe, Asia and North America. Only environmentally friendly materials have been used. The chair has been designed in such a way that waste, energy consumption and environmental impact are minimized. This makes »Think«, for which an environmental product declaration (EPD) has been drawn up, an environmentally friendly product throughout its entire life cycle.

But »Think« also does just that. It adapts intuitively to the body and its movements. Its back rest provides support to match the user's body weight and preferred work style. Its operating elements are simple to use. Its »Mein Komfort™ control«, for example, offers four settings for the amount of give in the back rest.

**Objektmöblierung
Silber**

**Contract furniture
Silver**

32 Seconds   **Arbeitsstuhl
Office chair**

Hersteller / Manufacturer
Steelcase Werndl AG
D-83026 Rosenheim

Design / Designer
Simon Wilkinson
C10 design & development bv
NL-2013 DK Haarlem

Vertrieb / Distributor
Steelcase Werndl AG
D-83026 Rosenheim

Jury
Herausragende ökologische Aspekte.
Dieser Stuhl ist wie alle anderen Steel-
case-Produkte sehr ökologisch und
zerlegbar. Steelcase hat eine herausragende Umweltpolitik und achtet bei der
Produktentwicklung und der Konstruktion, der Auswahl der Materialien sehr
auf Öko-Richtlinien. Gute Gestaltung.

Judges panel
Outstanding ecological aspects. Like
all other Steelcase products, this chair is
very ecological, and can be knocked
down. Steelcase's environmental policies
are excellent. In product development,
design and the choice of materials, it pays
great attention to ecological guidelines.
Good design.

»32 Seconds« ist in nur 32 Sekunden mit acht
einfachen Bedienelementen passend auf den Körper und die Aktivität des jeweiligen Nutzers
eingestellt. Er bietet effektiven Halt und einen einzigartigen Komfort für Rücken und Lendenwir-
belsäule. Die flexible Rückenlehne folgt den natürlichen Körperbewegungen und bietet damit
völlige Bewegungsfreiheit.

Den empfindlichen Lendenbereich unterstützen
zwei Innovationen: Die zwei UniFlex-Absorber
reagieren auf den Druck durch den Rücken und
schaffen so flexiblen Halt. Der Rückenlehnen-
träger bietet den ganzen Tag lang konstanten Halt
und verhindert so eine gekrümmte Sitzhaltung.

Bei seiner Entwicklung standen Nachhaltigkeit
und Umweltauswirkungen jedes Lebensab-
schnitts des Bürostuhls im Blickpunkt: Material-
gewinnung, Produktion, Transport, Verwendung und Wiederverwertung. Der Bürostuhl aus
umweltfreundlichen Materialien ist zu 99 Prozent recyclebar und kann mit handelsüblichem
Werkzeug in sechs Minuten zerlegt werden. Er
ist somit über seinen gesamten Lebenszyklus hinweg ein umweltschonender Stuhl, für den auch
eine Umweltprodukterklärung (EPD= Environmental Product Declaration) erstellt wurde.

The name »32 Seconds« is a reference to the time
it takes to adjust the chair to the user's physical
shape and activity, using eight simple adjusting
elements. It provides effective support and outstanding comfort for the back, especially the
small of the back. The flexible backrest follows the
natural movements of the body, and thus allows
complete freedom of movement.

Two innovations provide support for the lumbar
region: the two UniFlex absorbers react to pressure from the back, and in this way create flexible
support. The backrest brace provides constant
support throughout the day, in this way preventing
a hunched seating posture.

When developing this chair, the focus was on
the sustainability and environmental impact of
every stage of its life cycle: materials extraction,
production, transport, use and end-of-use strategies. Made of environmentally friendly materials, the office chair is 99 percent recyclable, and
can be knocked down in just six minutes using
conventional tools. This makes this chair, for which
an environmental product declaration (EPD) has
been drawn up, an environmentally friendly product throughout its entire life cycle.

144

Objektmöblierung
Silber

Contract furniture
Silver

Züco Riola **Konferenzsessel**
Conference chair

Hersteller / Manufacturer
Züco Bürositzmöbel AG
CH-9445 Rebstein

Design / Designer
Design Ballendat
Martin Ballendat
D-84359 Simbach

Vertrieb / Distributor
Dauphin
HumanDesign® Group GmbH & Co. KG
D-91238 Offenhausen

Jury
Zum einen kommt der Stuhl auf Grund der Bespannung mit diesem sehr interessanten Textilsitz mit extrem wenig Material aus. Zum zweiten halten wir den Stuhl für sehr, sehr langlebig im Design. Das führt dazu, dass so ein Stuhl nicht ständig wieder durch neue Stühle ersetzt werden muss, sondern dass er eine sehr lange Lebensdauer im Markt hat.

Judges panel
On the one hand, this chair makes do with very little material, due to its covering with this very interesting fabric. On the other hand, we feel that the chair's design makes it very, very long-lasting. This means that such a chair does not constantly have to be replaced by new chairs, but that it stays on the market for a very long time.

»Züco Riola« ist Drehsessel und Freischwinger in einem. Der Unterschied zum klassischen Vierfuß liegt einzig im Drehgelenk, das nicht wie üblich im Zentrum in der Nähe des Sitzes, sondern direkt über dem vierfüßigen Drehkreuz sitzt. Eine schräg gestellte Säule trägt den Schalensitz. Die Armlehnen wachsen optisch als Fortsetzung der Säule quasi aus dem Gestell heraus, was sein avantgardistisches Design unterstreicht.

Er besteht aus einem neuartigen patentierten und blickdichten Strickgewebe, das sich optimal dem Körper anpasst: dreidimensional verflochten bietet es unterschiedliche Härtezonen, was für hohen Komfort sorgt.

Es verbindet Elemente der Strick- und Webtechnik. Bei dieser Technologie wird die Form des Produkts digital abgenommen und in einem Arbeitsgang von der Maschine gestrickt. Das garantiert eine hohe Passgenauigkeit. Die klassische Zuschnitt- und Nähtechnik entfällt. Dadurch werden Energie- und Abfallkosten reduziert.

»Züco Riola« is a swivel chair and cantilever chair in one. The sole difference between this chair and the classic four-legged variety is its turning knuckle. This is not positioned centrally, directly under the seat, as is usual, but directly above the four-legged revolving base. An angled pillar supports the seat shell. The arm rests appear to grow out of the frame as an extension of the pillar. This emphasizes the chair's avant-garde design.

It uses an innovative, patented non-see-through knitted fabric that adapts excellently to the body: woven in three dimensions, it provides different hardness zones, and these make the chair so comfortable.

The way the fabric is made combines elements of knitting and weaving technology. In this technology, the shape of the product is recorded digitally and machine-knitted in one working cycle. This guarantees a high degree of accuracy. There is no need for the classic cutting and sewing processes, and this also reduces energy costs and waste.

146

Objektmöblierung **Contract furniture**
Silber **Silver**

Cinto **Stapelstuhl**
    Stackable chair

Hersteller / Manufacturer
Humanscale
New York, NY 10010
USA

Design / Designer
Humanscale Design Studio
Manuel Saez, Lachezar Tsvetanov, Emilian Dan Cartis
New York, NY 10001
USA

Vertrieb / Distributor
Bene Stuttgart
D-70565 Stuttgart

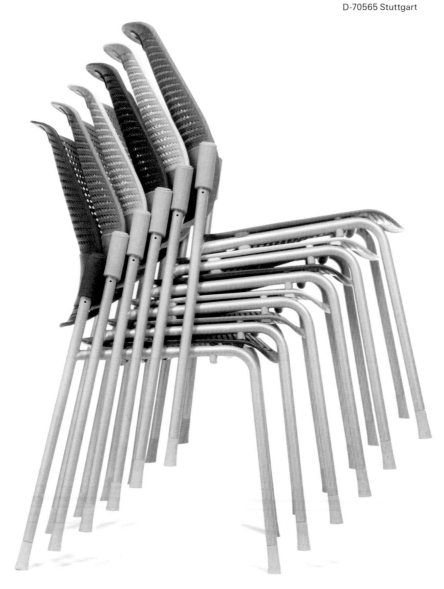

Jury
Ein preisgünstiger Stuhl, der durch zurückhaltenden Materialeinsatz überzeugt. Er ist hauptsächlich aus Polypropylen und Stahl. Auch die Konstruktion ist sehr ökologisch. Sie ermöglicht allein durch den Einsatz von Sitzschalen Federwirkung. Sehr gut. Eine intelligente Steckverbindung bei den Rollen: schnell demontierbar. Ökologie und Preis kombiniert – das überzeugt.

Judges panel
An inexpensive chair whose economical use of materials stands out. It is mainly made of polypropylene and steel. It is also very ecological in design. The seat pan on its own allows the seat the flex and bend. Very good. The way the casters can be attached is clever – quick to detach. Ecology and price in a convincing combination.

»Cinto« bietet beispiellosen Komfort und ungewöhnliche ergonomische Funktionen für einen Stuhl im günstigen Preissegment. Er ist so gestaltet, dass man sich bewegen kann und Druckstellen minimiert werden.

Sitzschale und Rückenlehne sind flexibel. Die Rückenlehne besitzt zusätzlich ein Band aus Elastomer, das den empfindlichen Lendenbereich unterstützt. Besondere Einschnitte in der Sitzschalenoberfläche verteilen das Gewicht und verringern Druckstellen.

»Cinto« gibt es in mehreren Varianten: mit und ohne Armlehnen, als Vierfüßer mit und ohne Rollen und als Freischwinger – und alle in verschiedenen Farben. Die Rollen lassen sich dank einer einfachen Steckverbindung schnell und bequem anbringen.

Um ihn leicht zu transportieren, ist in die Rückenlehne ein Griff integriert. Der Stuhl, der zu 100 Prozent recycelbar ist, besteht aus Stahl – für Beine und Rahmen – sowie aus Polypropylen – für Sitz und Rücken. Beim Stapelstuhl können bis zu 15 Exemplare übereinander gestapelt werden.

For a chair in the inexpensive price segment, »Cinto« offers unrivalled comfort and unusual ergonomic functions. It is designed so that the user can shift around in it, and so that pressure points are reduced.

The seat pan and backrest are flexible. The back rest also features an elastomer belt that supports the sensitive lumbar region. Special cutouts in the surface of the seat pan distribute weight and reduce pressure points.

»Cinto« is available in various models: with or without armrests, as a four-legged chair with or without casters, and as a cantilever chair – all of these models in various colours. Thanks to a simple connecting mechanism, the casters can be attached quickly and effortlessly.

To make the chair easy to transport, a handle has been integrated into the backrest. The 100 percent recyclable chair is made of steel (legs and frame) and polypropylene (seat and back). Up to 15 chairs can be stacked on top of each other.

148

Objektmöblierung   **Contract furniture**
Silber   **Silver**

Kalidro   **Büroarbeitstisch**
              Office desk

              Hersteller / Manufacturer
              Steelcase Werndl AG
              D-83026 Rosenheim

              Design / Designer
              Brodbeck Design
              D-80336 München

              Vertrieb / Distributor
              Steelcase Werndl AG
              D-83026 Rosenheim

Jury

Dieser Tisch besitzt einige Elemente, die ökologischer sind als bei vergleichbaren Produkten anderer Firmen, wie zum Beispiel: Die Kanten sind mit einem Klebstoff auf Wasserbasis umleimt. Es wird recyceltes Aluminium eingesetzt. Es werden polierte Aluminiumteile anstatt verchromte Teile benutzt. Die Stahlteile sind pulverbeschichtet. Insgesamt ein materialreduzierter, schlichter, langlebiger Tisch.

Judges panel

The desk comprises a number of elements that are more ecological than in the products of other companies. For example, the edge bands are glued with a water-based adhesive. Recycled aluminium is used. The aluminium parts used are polished instead of chrome plated. The steel parts are powder coated. All in all, a simple, long-lasting desk that gets by with less material.

Der höhenverstellbare Tisch zeichnet sich durch seine reduzierte, zeitlose Gestaltung mit einem farblich kontrastierenden Rahmen aus. Mit einem polierten Fußanbinder lassen sich verschiedene Akzente setzen.

Wie bei allen Steelcase-Produkten wurden auch beim Entwicklungsprozess von »Kalidro« die Umweltauswirkungen aller Phasen des Produkt-Lebenszyklus – von der Rohstoff-Gewinnung über die Produktion, den Transport, die Verwendung und das Recycling bis hin zur Entsorgung – berücksichtigt.

So ist der mit dem Blauen Engel zertifizierte Tisch zu 34 Prozent aus recyceltem Material hergestellt und zu 99 Prozent recycelbar. Und das verwendete Holz stammt aus nachhaltiger Forstwirtschaft. Es wurde, wo möglich, Material eingespart, beispielsweise durch dünnere Tischplatten. Holzabfälle aus dem Plattenzuschnitt werden vom Lieferanten wiederverwendet, um Spanplatten zu produzieren. Die Eckknoten bestehen aus 100 Prozent recyceltem Aluminium. Seit Produkteinführung konnten weitere 100 Gramm Aluminium je Eckknoten eingespart werden. Dank einer speziellen Rahmenkonstruktion wird Stahlabfall nahezu komplett vermieden.

This height-adjustable desk features a reduced, timeless design and a colour-contrasting frame. The polished connecting pieces between desk top and legs are a further attractive feature.

As with all Steelcase products, when developing Kalidro the environmental impact of every phase of the product life-cycle was considered – from extraction and production of raw materials, via production, transport and use, to recycling and disposal.

For example, this desk, which carries the »Blue Angel« German environment label, is made of 34 percent recycled materials, and is 99 percent recyclable. And the wood that is used comes from sustainable forestry. Wherever possible, materials have been used sparingly – by using thinner desktops, for example. The supplier uses any wood waste that arises from cutting the desktops to size to produce chipboard. The corner nodes are made of 100 percent recycled aluminium. Since the product was launched, a further 100 grams of aluminium per corner node have been saved. Thanks to a special frame design, practically no steel is wasted.

152

Kommunikation
Gold

**Communication
Gold**

Growing Table   **Mitwachsender Kindertisch und Bank
Height-adjustable children's desk and bench**

Hersteller / Manufacturer
Pure Position
D-60327 Frankfurt

Design / Designer
Werksdesign / In-house design
Olaf Schroeder

Vertrieb / Distributor
Pure Position
D-60327 Frankfurt

Jury
Die ideale Lösung für ein Kind. Interessant ist das System mit den Beinen. Tisch, Bank und Hocker wachsen mit, können also lange verwendet werden. Ein sehr einfaches, ehrliches Produkt. Sehr schöne Idee: die verschiedenen Tools, die in die Tischplatte gesteckt werden können.

Judges panel
The ideal solution for a child. The system with the legs is interesting. Desk, bench and stool grow with the child, and so can be used for a long time. A very simple, honest product. Very good idea: the various accessories that can be inserted into the desktop.

Die Beine von Tisch, Hocker und Bank lassen sich dank eines unkomplizierten Schraubmechanismus mit nur drei Teilen auf vier verschiedene Höhen einstellen. So kann das mitwachsende Möbel-Set für Kinder ab zwei Jahren bis ins Jugendalter verwendet werden. Nicht nur der lange Nutzungszeitraum macht es nachhaltig, sondern zudem bewirken die Konstruktion, die an historische robuste Bauernmöbel erinnert, und das schlichte, zurückhaltende Design eine visuelle Langlebigkeit.

Volumige, leicht diagonal ausgerichtete Beine aus heimischer Buche massiv halten die 25 Millimeter starken Platten. Das macht die Möbel sehr stabil und gibt ihnen ihr typisches, sympathisches Aussehen. Tischplatte und Auflagen für Bank und Hocker bestehen aus klar lackierten Buche-Multiplexplatten in natur oder farbig gebeizt. Der Tisch besitzt Lochreihen, in die das Kind Bücherboard, Buchaufsteller, Zettel- oder Stiftebox stecken, beliebig anordnen und so selbst für Ordnung sorgen kann. Eine integrierbare Zeichenrolle lädt zur kreativen Beschäftigung allein oder zu mehreren ein.

Produziert wird »growing table« ausschließlich in Deutschland in einer Behinderten-Werkstatt. Hier werden alle Teile gefertigt, konfektioniert und ausgeliefert. Selbst die dazugehörigen Druckerzeugnisse stellt man in der Druckerei des Herstellers her. Damit wurde eine hohe Fertigungstiefe erreicht, die Wege und Ressourcen spart.

The desk, stool and bench legs can be adjusted to four different heights, thanks to an uncomplicated screw mechanism comprising just three parts. The furniture set grows as the children grow, and can be used from the age of two until adolescence. It is not only this long period of use that makes it sustainable. The way it is put together, which is reminiscent of historical, sturdy rustic furniture, and its plain, unassuming design give a visual impression of longevity.

The 25 millimetre thick desk top is supported by chunky, slightly diagonal legs made of solid, locally grown beech. This makes the furniture very sturdy, and gives it its typical pleasant appearance. The desktop and seat surfaces for the bench and stool are made of transparent varnished multiplex beech, either natural or stained. Rows of holes have been drilled into the desk, into which the child can plug a book shelf, book rest, note box and pencil box as desired, and in this way keep the desk tidy. For creative activities, either alone or with others, there is an integrated roll of drawing paper.

The »growing table« is made exclusively in Germany, in a disabled persons' workshop. All the parts are produced, put together and dispatched here. Even the print products that are needed for the desk are made in the manufacturer's own print shop. This results in a high degree of manufacturing depth, which saves transport and resources.

Kommunikation   **Communication**
Silber   **Silver**

Green Collection   **Holzstifte**
                         Wooden writing implements

                         Hersteller / Manufacturer
                         Stabilo International GmbH
                         D-90562 Heroldsberg

                         Design / Designer
                         Ideenhaus Kommunikationsagentur GmbH
                         D-90402 Nürnberg

                         Vertrieb / Distributor
                         Stabilo International GmbH
                         Vertriebsbüro Deutschland
                         D-90562 Heroldsberg

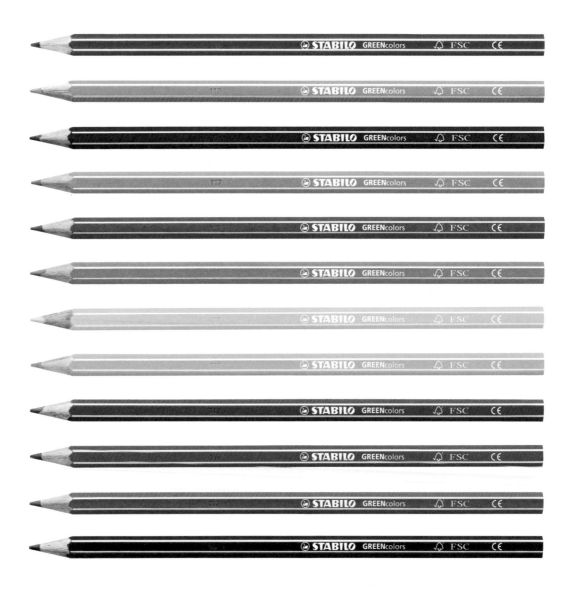

Jury
Das Holz kommt aus FSC-zertifizierten Quellen, ist also nachhaltig bewirtschaftet. Es gibt bestimmte soziale Aspekte in der Produktion, die berücksichtigt werden. Die Verpackung ist aus Altpapier, also aus Recycling-Karton. Insgesamt eine sehr konsequente und auch optisch ansprechende Lösung. Interessant, weil damit auch Kindern das Thema »Umweltschutz« kommuniziert wird.

Judges panel
The wood comes from FSC-certified sources, which means it is managed sustainably, and production respects certain social aspects. The packaging is made of recycled cardboard. All in all, a very uncompromising solution, but at the same time a visually attractive one. Interesting because it communicates the subject of environmental protection to children.

Die Serie besteht aus Leuchtmarkierern, Farb- und Bleistiften – ideal für die LOHAS (Lifestyle of health and sustainability). Diese Gruppe, die in Europa und den USA stark wächst, achtet neben hoher Qualität auch auf Nachhaltigkeit und Gesundheit.

Stabilo hat sich schon sehr früh auf das steigende Umweltbewusstsein eingestellt und kontinuierlich Produktions- und Arbeitsbedingungen optimiert. Alle drei Stifte sind FSC (Forest Stewardship Council) zertifiziert. Das bedeutet, dass das Holz der Stifte zu 100 Prozent aus ökologisch und sozial vorbildlich bewirtschafteten Wäldern kommt – nur aus nachwachsenden Beständen und nicht aus Kriegsgebieten. In diesen Wäldern müssen aktive Schutzmaßnahmen für bedrohte Pflanzen und Tiere, für Wasserreservoirs und Bodenerosion ergriffen werden. Darüber hinaus müssen die Interessen der Ureinwohner respektiert werden.

Alle Stifte sind mit einem umweltfreundlichen Mattlack lackiert.

This series comprises markers, crayons and pencils – ideal for the LOHAS (lifestyle of health and sustainability) market segment. This consumer segment, which is growing strongly in Europe and the U.S., places great importance on high quality, sustainability and health.

Stabilo geared its operations very early to the trend towards more environmental awareness, and has continuously optimized its production and working conditions. All three implements are certified by the Forest Stewardship Council (FSC). This means that the wood used to make them comes from forests that are managed completely ecologically and to the highest social standards – only from renewable stocks and not from war zones. In these forests, active measures must be taken to protect endangered plants and animals, as well as to protect water resources and control erosion. In addition, the interests of indigenous peoples have to be respected.

All the writing implements are treated with eco-friendly matt paint.

156

Kommunikation **Communication**
Silber **Silver**

Lamy noto **Kugelschreiber**
Ballpoint pen

Hersteller / Manufacturer
C. Josef Lamy GmbH
D-69123 Heidelberg

Design / Designer
Naoto Fukasawa
Shibuya-KV Tokyo 150-0001
Japan

Vertrieb / Distributor
C. Josef Lamy GmbH
D-69123 Heidelberg

Jury
Schlichter, schöner, gut gestalteter, ganz einfacher Kugelschreiber in einer sehr niedrigen Preiskategorie. Er ist so schön, dass er sicherlich kein Wegwerfstift ist. Man wird sich bei ihm die Mühe machen, die Mine auszutauschen und ihn behalten. Ein überzeugendes Produkt.

Judges panel
Unassuming, elegant, well designed, very simple ballpoint pen in a very low price category. It is so attractive that it cannot be a disposable pen. With a design like this, people will always make the effort to get a refill so that they can keep the pen. A product that makes sense.

»Lamy noto« zeichnet sich durch die konsequente Reduktion seiner Form auf das Notwendigste aus. Der Kugelschreiber ist für den täglichen und häufigen Einsatz gedacht und im niedrigen Preissegment angesiedelt. Er beschränkt sich auf die wesentlichen Funktionen und das gute Schreiben.

Das moderne und attraktive Design wird durch den in die Gehäusekontur integrierten Clip noch unterstrichen. Der dreieckige Körper mit seinen weichen Kanten liegt federleicht in der Hand. Die matte Oberfläche verleiht ihm einen samtenen Eindruck.

Der einfache Kunststoffkugelschreiber ist in den Farben schwarz, hellgrau, blau, orange und in iceblue zu erhalten. Außerdem gibt es eine Ausführung aus besonders schwerem Kunststoff in schwarz mit Spitze und Drücker mattsilbern lackiert.

What is striking about »Lamy noto« is that its form has consistently been reduced to the bare minimum. The ballpoint pen is designed for frequent everyday use, and is positioned in the low-price segment. It has been restricted to its essential functions and ease of writing.

Its modern and attractive design is further underscored by the clip, which is integrated into the contours of the body. Its triangular body with its soft edges is light as a feather to hold. Its matt surface creates a velvet-like impression.

This simple, plastic ballpoint is available in black, light grey, blue, orange and ice-blue. There is also a version made of especially heavy black plastic, with a matt-silver tip and push-button.

158

Kommunikation **Communication**
Silber **Silver**

Connect 37 **Media Full-HD+ inkl. DR+**
Media Full-HD+ incl. DR+

Hersteller / Manufacturer
Loewe Opta GmbH
D-96317 Kronach

Design / Designer
Design 3
D-20459 Hamburg

Vertrieb / Distributor
Loewe Opta GmbH
D-96317 Kronach

Der »Connect 37« ist der multimediale Mittelpunkt im Wohnzimmer und vereinigt in einem einzigen Gerät: Fernseher, Radio, Festplattenrecorder, Netzwerk-Mediaplayer und Common Interface zum Empfang verschlüsselter Sender (z. B. Premiere) sowie digitaler Fernseh-Empfänger für alle gängigen Standards wie Antenne, Kabel oder Satellit. So zeigt er auch Fotos und Filme per Funknetzwerk vom PC und das in hochauflösender Bild- und Klangqualität.

Man spart nicht nur die Gehäuse der sonst notwendigen Einzelgeräte, zusätzliche Fernbedienungen und Elektronikkomponenten wie zum Beispiel Netzteile, sondern auch Energie bei der Herstellung. Es wurden keine Gehäuseteile mit halogenhaltigen Flammhemmern verwendet. Trotz des Hochglanzdesigns sind die Gehäuseteile nicht lackiert. Er lässt sich an der Unterseite abschalten und verbraucht so keinen Strom. Im Stand-by-Modus wird nur ein Watt aufgenommen.

Seine moderne, zeitlose Gestaltung, die Materialauswahl und die hochwertige Verarbeitung sind auf Langlebigkeit ausgelegt. Für das spätere Recycling wurden die Kunststoffe eigens gekennzeichnet.

»Connect 37« is the multimedia focus in the living room. In one and the same appliance, it combines the functions of television, radio, hard-disk recorder, home network media player and common interface for the reception of encoded channels, as well as functioning as a digital television receiver for all the common standards such as aerial, cable or satellite. It can also show photographs and films transmitted by radio from a PC – and this in high-resolution image and sound quality.

This not only saves the space taken up by the appliances that would otherwise be necessary, but also means there is no need for extra remote controls and electrical components such as mains units. Moreover, it saves energy in the manufacturing process. No halogens have been used when fireproofing the parts of the housing. Despite its high-gloss design, the housing parts are not varnished. A switch on the underside of the appliance means that it consumes no electricity when switched off. In stand-by, it consumes just one watt.

Its modern, timeless design, the choice of materials and the high-quality finish are all intended to make this a long-lasting appliance. For subsequent recycling, the different plastics used are marked accordingly.

Focus in Gold

Eva Solo   Thermos-Wasserflasche
Thermo Water Flask

162

Freizeit und Outdoor
Gold

Leisure and outdoor activities
Gold

Eva Solo   **Thermos-Wasserflasche**
Thermo Water Flask

Hersteller / Manufacturer
Eva Denmark A/S
DK-2760 Måløv

Design / Designer
Tools Design®
Claus Jensen & Henrik Holbæk
DK-2400 Kopenhagen NV

Vertrieb / Distributor
Eva Denmark A/S
DK-2760 Måløv

Jury
Sehr schöne Alternative zur Kunststoff-
flasche. Vielleicht führt sie auch dazu,
dass Leute weniger Wasser in Kunststoff-
flaschen kaufen und es lieber direkt
aus dem Wasserhahn mitnehmen. Wunderschöne Interpretation einer Flasche,
klare Form. Einfacher geht es gar nicht.
Und ein langlebiges Material – Edelstahl.

Judges panel
Very elegant alternative to the plastic
bottle. Perhaps it will also result in people
buying less water in plastic bottles and
taking it with them direct from the tap instead. Beautiful interpretation of a bottle, clear form. Things don't come simpler
than this. And a long-lasting material –
stainless steel.

In die Thermos-Wasserflasche kann man kaltes
Wasser füllen und beispielsweise auf Ausflügen
oder Reisen mitnehmen. Dank einer im Deckel
integrierten Schlaufe lässt sich die Flasche ganz
bequem am Handgelenk tragen. Damit hat man
unterwegs immer eine kühle Erfrischung dabei.

Hinter der Thermos-Wasserflasche steckt die
Idee, den Gebrauch von Kunststoff-Wasserfla-
schen, wo es möglich ist, zu ersetzen. Außerdem muss das Wasser, dadurch dass es in der
Thermosflasche kühl gehalten wird, nicht immer wieder von neuem gekühlt werden. Die Ver-
schwendung von Trinkwasser wird reduziert,
weil das Wasser in der Thermosflasche frisch gehalten wird.

Die Wasserflasche besteht aus doppelwandigem
Edelstahl und ist damit eine echte Thermosflasche. Sie ist spülmaschinenfest, lediglich der
Schraubdeckel mit Riemen muss von Hand gespült werden.

The water flask can be filled with cold water and
taken on trips or journeys, for example. Thanks
to a strap integrated in the lid, the flask can com-
fortably be carried around the wrist. And so a
cool, refreshing drink is always available when
you're on the move.

The idea behind the Thermo water flask is to do
without plastic water bottles wherever possible.
Moreover, because it is kept cool in the flask, the
water does not constantly have to be re-cooled.
The waste of drinking water is reduced, because
the water is kept fresh in the flask.

The flask is made of double-walled stainless steel,
making it a true thermo flask. It is dishwasher-safe:
only the screw lid and strap have to be washed
by hand.

164

Freizeit und Outdoor
Silber

Leisure and outdoor activities
Silver

Macharten Lederkollektion

**Taschen
Bags**

Hersteller / Manufacturer
Macharten
D-76137 Karlsruhe

Design / Designer
Werksdesign / In-house design
Monika Assem

Vertrieb / Distributor
Macharten
D-76137 Karlsruhe

Jury
Die Taschen sind aus einem sehr schönen Material, aus massivem Leder, das
auf lange Sicht hin patiniert wird. Sie
sind keine Wegwerf-Modeartikel, sondern haben eine hohe Langlebigkeit.
Sie sind sehr schön in der Form und spre-
chen emotional an.

Judges panel
The bags are made of a beautiful material, real leather, which will take on a patina as the years go by. They are not
throw-away fashion articles, but are designed to last for a long time. Their form
is very elegant, and they appeal to the
emotions.

Die Taschen sind sinnlich und puristisch zugleich.
Puristisch durch ihre reduzierten eleganten und
zeitlosen Formen. Sinnlich durch ihre angenehme
und besondere Haptik des Rindsleders, das
schonend im Kastanienholzfass gegerbt wird.
Zusammen mit den schlichten Metallbeschlägen
erhalten die hochwertigen Taschen ihre span-
nungsvolle und anziehende Ästhetik.

Die verschiedenen Modelle werden in einer deutschen Ledermanufaktur in aufwendiger Handarbeit gefertigt. Dabei wird sehr großer Wert auf
die handverlesene Auswahl und sparsame Verarbeitung der eingesetzten Rohmaterialien gelegt.

These bags are sensual and purist at the same
time. Purist because of their reduced forms,
which are elegant and timeless. Sensual because
of the pleasant, special feel of the cow leather,
which is gently tanned in a chestnut barrel. Together with their plain metal fittings, this gives
the high-quality bags an exciting and attractive
aesthetic quality.

The various models are hand made in a German
leatherware workshop. Great importance is
placed on the careful selection of the raw materials used, and on processing them economically.

Kamerad Tasche
Bag

Freizeit und Outdoor **Leisure and outdoor activities**
Silber **Silver**

Kamerad **Tasche**
Bag

Hersteller / Manufacturer
Lemonfish® GmbH
D-73655 Plüderhausen

Design / Designer
Werksdesign / In-house design

Vertrieb / Distributor
Lemonfish® GmbH
D-73655 Plüderhausen

Jury
Es ist ein soziales Thema: die Wiederverwendung von altem Material und die Bearbeitung im Frauengefängnis. Es hat großen Charme, mit alten Armeematerialien so umzugehen und dann auch noch eine Blümchen-Dekoration darauf zu setzen. Man spielt hier mit Witz und Ironie. Und das ist sehr schön.

Judges panel
A social topic: the re-use of old materials and their processing in a women's prison. The way these old army materials are treated is very charming, especially with the flowers that are added as decoration. This is playful, witty and ironic. And that's what is so good about these bags.

Für alle Taschenmodelle werden Details und Materialien von robusten, gebrauchten Seesäcken der Bundeswehr zusammen mit originalen Stoffen der 1960er und 1970er Jahre verarbeitet und verwertet. Das kräftige Baumwollmaterial und die ursprünglichen Aluminiumdetails machen die Taschen unempfindlich.

Jede Tasche ist ein Unikat. Patina, Gebrauchsspuren und reparierte Stellen werden mit einem funktionalen Innenleben kombiniert. Die neue, weiche und praktische Einteilung bildet einen schönen Kontrast zu dem gebrauchten Äußeren.

Hergestellt werden die »Kameraden« in einem nahegelegenen Frauengefängnis. Dort werden die ursprünglichen Seesäcke gereinigt und anschließend die Taschen genäht. So sind nur kurze Wege nötig.

For all these bag models, the details and materials of robust, used German army kitbags have been recycled and used, together with original materials from the 1960s and 1970s. The robust cotton fabric and the original aluminium details mean that the bags are hard-wearing.

Every bag is a unique article. Patina, traces of previous use and places where the material has been mended go hand in hand with a functional interior. Its new, soft and practical compartments contrast beautifully with the used exterior.

The »Kameraden« bags are made in a women's prison near by. The original kitbags are washed there, and the bags are then sewn together. The whole production process only involves short distances, therefore.

168

Nautiloop **Aufrollbare Tasche
Shopping bag to go**

Hersteller / Manufacturer
DNS-Designteam
D-10999 Berlin

Design / Designer
Werksdesign / In-house design

Vertrieb / Distributor
DNS-Designteam
D-10999 Berlin

Jury
Kunststofftüten schaden der Umwelt. Hier versucht man dagegen ein neues Mittel zu kommunizieren. Der ökologische Aspekt besteht darin, dass man durch so eine einfach mitnehmbare, immer wieder verwendbare Tasche Kunststofftüten vermeidet.

Judges panel
Plastic bags are bad for the environment. Here is an attempt to communicate this through a new medium. What is ecological about it is that by having a bag that can always be reused and is simple to take with you, plastic bags can be avoided.

Häufig benötigt man spontan eine Tasche und hat gerade keine dabei: Beim Reisen oder auf Messen beispielsweise oder wenn man nach der Arbeit noch schnell etwas einkaufen möchte. Dann greift man meist zur Wegwerf-Plastiktüte.

»Nautiloop« ist eine wiederverwendbare und nachhaltige Tasche, die Wegwerfplastiktüten ersetzt. Wenn man die Tasche nicht braucht, wird sie in einem robusten Gehäuse aufgerollt. So lässt sie sich einfach und praktisch mitnehmen.

Benötigt man »Nautiloop« – »nautilus« bedeutet Meeresschnecke und »loop« Kreislauf –, zieht man an der Schlaufe, und eine große strapazierfähige Schultertasche »entwickelt« sich. Nach Gebrauch lässt sie sich ganz einfach wieder in ihr Gehäuse zurückdrehen. Ein weiteres praktisches Detail ist der integrierte Einkaufswagenchip.

Das Gehäuse ist aus Polycarbonat, das zu 100 Prozent recycelbar ist. Die Tasche ist entweder in Seide oder in langlebigem Polyester-Stoff zu haben.

There are many occasions when you quickly need a bag but don't have one with you: when travelling or at trade fairs, for example, or when you need to buy something quickly on the way home from work. Most of us then make do with a disposable plastic bag.

»Nautiloop« is a re-usable, long-lasting bag that replaces disposable plastic bags. When it is not needed, it is rolled into a sturdy case. This makes it simple and practical to take with you.

If you need »Nautiloop« – its name is taken from the nautilus mollusc – all you have to do is pull on the loop, and a large, hard-wearing shoulder bag »unravels«. After use, it is simply rewound into its case. One further practical detail is the integrated chip for shopping trolleys.

The case is made of polycarbonate, which is 100 percent recyclable. The bag is available in silk or long-lasting polyester.

170

Freizeit und Outdoor
Silber

Leisure and outdoor activities
Silver

Grashopper **Freizeitschuh**
Leisure shoe

Hersteller / Manufacturer
Sioux GmbH
D-74399 Walheim

Design / Designer
Werksdesign / In-house design
Reinhold Schulz

Vertrieb / Distributor
Kuball & Kempe
D-20457 Hamburg

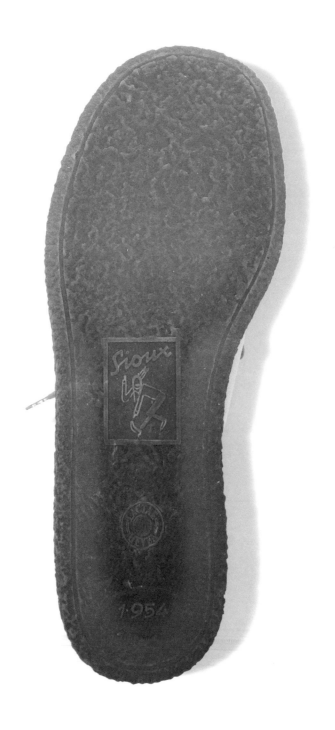

Jury
Eines der konsequentesten ökologischen Produkte des Wettbewerbs. Mit rhabarbergegerbtem Leder, die Sohle ist aus Naturkautschuk, alles ist handwerklich, also per Hand gefertigt in Deutschland. Qualitativ hochwertig, ein phantastisches Laufgefühl. Gut zu Menschen, zur Umwelt, ästhetisch ein Designklassiker.

Judges panel
One of the most uncompromisingly ecological products of the competition. With rhubarb-tanned leather, a sole made of natural rubber, everything is crafted, made by hand in Germany. High quality, a fantastic walking sensation. Good for people and the environment, aesthetically a design classic.

»Grashopper« ist ein Klassiker und hat sich zum Kultschuh entwickelt. Mit seiner anatomischen Passform bietet er hohen Geh- und Tragekomfort.

Er zeichnet sich durch seine hervorragende Qualität und schadstoffarme Substanzen aus. So besteht er aus rhabarbergegerbtem Bio-Leder, das nicht, wie häufig üblich, durch eine Kunststoffschicht versiegelt wird. Dadurch kann das Leder atmen und sich schnell der Raumtemperatur anpassen. Das führt nicht nur zu einem warmen angenehmen und geschmeidigen Gefühl bei Berührung, sondern auch die Fußfeuchtigkeit wird dadurch schnell aufgenommen und wieder abgegeben, was einem Wärme- und Feuchtigkeitsstau entgegenwirkt.

Neben den pflanzlichen Gerbstoffen sind auch die anderen »Herstellungs-Zutaten« gesundheitlich und ökologisch unbedenklich, wie synthetische Farbstoffe sowie native Öle und Fette. Produziert wird ausschließlich in Deutschland.

Die Kautschuksohlen werden, wie sie die Indianer in Südamerika gefertigt hatten, ausschließlich aus der Milch des Hevea-Baums einzeln und von Hand hergestellt. Ähnlich dem Prozess der Käseherstellung wird die Milch gefiltert, in Formen gegossen, wo sie gerinnt. Während der Trocknung entstehen tausende von Luftbläschen in der Sohle.

Das alles führt zum unvergleichlichen Tragekomfort, zu höchster Elastizität und Geschmeidigkeit.

The »Grashopper« is a classic that has become a cult shoe. With its anatomic form, it is comfortable to wear and to walk in.

Its main characteristics are excellent quality and low-polluting substances. For example, it is made of rhubarb-tanned organic leather, which is not sealed with a plastic coat as is very often the case. This allows the leather to breathe, and to adjust quickly to ambient temperature. This not only makes it warm, pleasant and supple to the touch, but also means that perspiration is quickly absorbed and released again, preventing heat and moisture from building up.

Apart from the vegetable tanning agents, the other materials used in the shoe's manufacture are good for the health and the environment, such as the synthetic dyes and native oil and fat. The shoe is made exclusively in Germany.

The rubber soles are made individually and by hand, using only the latex of the hevea tree, just as they were made by the South American Indians. In a process similar to cheese-making, the latex is filtered and poured into moulds, where it cures. During the drying process, thousands of tiny air bubbles form in the sole.

All of this results in unrivalled comfort, extreme elasticity and suppleness.

**Freizeit und Outdoor
Silber**

**Leisure and outdoor activities
Silver**

**Eva Solo   Nistkasten
Nesting box**

Hersteller / Manufacturer
Eva Denmark A/S
DK-2760 Måløv

Design / Designer
Tools Design®
Claus Jensen & Henrik Holbæk
DK-2400 Kopenhagen NV

Vertrieb / Distributor
Eva Denmark A/S
DK-2760 Måløv

Jury
Das Porzellanvogelhäuschen animiert auch Freunde puristischer Gestaltung dazu, Vögeln ein Heim zu geben. Designer haben sich dieses Themas angenommen, es ist ein sehr schön designtes Vogelhaus mit einer außergewöhnlichen Gestaltung herausgekommen. Und es ist vogelfreundlich. Es wird von Vögeln gerne bewohnt.

Judges panel
This terracotta nesting box will inspire lovers of purist design to give birds a home. Designers have busied themselves with this topic, and have come up with a beautifully styled nesting box with an unusual design. And it's bird-friendly, too. Birds will readily build their nests in it.

Einige Vogelgruppen können ihre Nester nur in Hohlräumen bauen, wie sie sie beispielsweise in alten Baumstämmen finden. Aber in der modernen Welt wird es für sie immer schwieriger, solche geeigneten Hohlräume zum Nisten zu finden. Da können Menschen helfen, indem sie Nistkästen aufstellen, und so ein Stück Natur schützen.

Dieses Exemplar eines Nistkastens sticht durch seine außergewöhnliche moderne Gestaltung hervor, die sich durch Klarheit und minimalistische Reduktion auszeichnet.

Der Nistkasten besteht aus Keramik, die über gute Wärmeeigenschaften verfügt. Die Oberfläche ist glasiert und reflektiert das Sonnenlicht.

Der Deckel des Nistkastens besitzt eine Leiter, die in den Nistkasten führt. Die Sprossen können die Vögel mit ihren Krallen umfassen. Damit ist gewährleistet, dass die Vögel und später auch die Jungvögel aus dem Nistkasten herauskommen können.

Some species of birds can only build their nests in cavities such as those found in old tree trunks. But in the modern world, it is becoming more and more difficult for them to find suitable cavities for nesting. People can help here by putting up nesting boxes, and in this way conserve part of the natural world.

The design of this nesting box is unusually modern. It is strikingly clear, and reduced to the minimum.

It is made of a terracotta ceramic that has good heat properties. The surface is glazed, and reflects the sunlight.

The lid of the nesting box has a ladder that leads into the box. Birds can grip its rungs with their claws. This ensures that the birds, and later the fledglings, can climb out of the box again.

RazorCut Spindelmäher
Cylinder mower

Freizeit und Outdoor
Silber

Leisure and outdoor activities
Silver

RazorCut   **Spindelmäher**
Cylinder mower

Hersteller / Manufacturer
Brill Gloria
Haus- und Gartengeräte GmbH
D-58456 Witten

Design / Designer
Weinberg & Ruf
Produktgestaltung
D-70794 Filderstadt

Vertrieb / Distributor
Brill Gloria
Haus- und Gartengeräte GmbH
Vertriebs- und Marketingzentrale
D-89231 Neu-Ulm

Jury
Der Rasenmäher wird manuell betrieben und verbraucht weder Strom noch Treibstoff. Das ist ökologisch sehr sinnvoll. Es ist schön zu sehen, dass manuelle Rasenmäher wieder populär werden. Außerdem ist es die bessere Art, Gras zu mähen, da das Gras nicht gequetscht, sondern richtig geschnitten wird, das heißt, es wächst besser und die Rasenoberfläche sieht besser aus.

Judges panel
This lawn mower is manually operated, and uses neither electricity nor fuel. This makes a lot of ecological sense. It is good to see manual lawn mowers becoming popular again. Apart from that, it is a better way of mowing grass, since the grass is not crushed but cut properly. This means it grows better, and the lawn looks better.

Der Klassiker unter den Rasenmähern erscheint hier in neuem Design. Die moderne Form des robusten und dennoch einfach zusammenklappbaren Holms in Silber und Grau mit ergonomischem Moosgummigriff besticht. Für komfortables Arbeiten lässt sich der Holm in der Höhe frei einstellen.

Mit diesem Spindelmäher lässt sich das Gras zum gepflegten, englischen Rasen trimmen und gleichzeitig die Umwelt und die Stromrechnung schonen.

Die von Brill erfundene kontaktfreie Schneidtechnik sorgt für geräuscharmes Arbeiten und einen präzisen Schnitt. Der auf ein hundertstel Millimeter genaue Präzisionsschliff von Messerwalze und Untermesser aus gehärtetem Spezialstahl hinterlässt einen Rasen, der wie mit der Schere geschnitten zu sein scheint.

Der Rasenmäher ist besonders bedienerfreundlich. Das breite, für unterschiedliche Rasenarten entwickelte Radprofil überträgt die Kraft zum Antrieb der Spindel. Ein Leitprofil an der Haube lenkt den Grasauswurf kontrolliert nach hinten.

A classic lawnmower in a new design. Its striking feature is the modern form of the sturdy, yet easy to fold down handle bar, in silver and grey, with foam rubber handles. For ease of use, the handle can be adjusted to any height.

Using this cylinder mower, grass can be trimmed to a manicured lawn, and it is good for the environment and the electricity bill as well.

The non-contact cutting technique invented by Brill allows mowing to be done in silence, and makes for a precise cut. Precision sharpened to a hundredth of a millimetre, blade cylinder and bottom blade of special hardened steel leave the lawn looking as though it has been cut with scissors.

The lawn mower is especially user-friendly. The large wheels with their special profile developed for different types of lawns transfer force to drive the reel. A spoiler on the hood ejects the grass cuttings in a controlled manner.

SBP 3800 Fasspumpe
Submersible pump

Freizeit und Outdoor
Silber

Leisure and outdoor activities
Silver

SBP 3800 **Fasspumpe**
Submersible pump

Hersteller / Manufacturer
Alfred Kärcher GmbH & Co. KG
D-71364 Winnenden

Design / Designer
Werksdesign / In-house design
Michael Meyer
und
B/F Industrial Design
Christoph Böhler
D-90419 Nürnberg

Vertrieb / Distributor
Alfred Kärcher Vertriebs-GmbH
D-71364 Winnenden

Jury
Eine Regenwasserpumpe ist schon per se ökologisch. Es gibt sie zwar schon lange, aber Kärcher erweitert hier das System, indem man einen Schwimmerschalter hat, die Pumpe besonders energieeffizient ist und man auch einen normalen Gartenschlauch daran anschließen kann. Insofern wird es erleichtert, Regenwasser im Garten zum Gießen zu benutzen. Überzeugendes Produkt.

Judges panel
A submersible pump is in itself ecological, and is something that has been around for some time. Here, Kärcher has extended the system by providing a float switch, by making the pump especially energy efficient, and by making it possible to attach a normal garden hose. This makes it easier to use rainwater for watering the garden. Impressive product.

Die Fasspumpe leistet auf Grund ihrer hohen Energieeffizienz einen Beitrag zum Klimaschutz. Sie hilft beim Sparen von Trinkwasser, denn Regenwasser kann mit ihrer Hilfe zum Gießen von Beeten und Rasenflächen eingesetzt werden. Zudem schont Regenwasser im Gegensatz zu Leitungswasser die Blumen. Und sie ist sehr viel komfortabler als Gießkannen. Einfach einen Gartenschlauch und eine Spritze anschließen und bewässern.

Die »SBP 3800« kann dank eines ausgeklügelten Systems variabel in Fässern unterschiedlicher Größe benutzt werden: Anstatt eines starren Anschlussrohrs verfügt sie nämlich über einen flexiblen Schlauch. Ihr Schwimmerschalter dient auch – eingefügt in eine Klemmvorrichtung – als Ein- und Ausschalter. Damit kann die Fasspumpe sofort nach Gebrauch am Gerät selbst ausgeschaltet werden.

Umweltaspekte wurden von Beginn an im Produktentstehungsprozess berücksichtigt. So wurden beispielsweise alle Kunststoffteile mit ihrer Materialart gekennzeichnet, um das Recycling zu erleichtern.

With its high level of energy efficiency, this submersible pump helps protect the climate. It helps to save drinking water, since it allows rainwater to be used to water flower beds and lawns. Unlike tap water, moreover, rainwater is kind to flowers. And the pump is much easier to use than a watering can. Simply connect a hose pipe and a nozzle, and watering can start.

Thanks to a sophisticated system, the »SBP 3800« can be used in different sizes of vats. Instead of a rigid connecting pipe, it has a flexible hose. Integrated in a clamping device, the float switch is also an on/off switch. This allows the pump to be switched off at the appliance itself immediately after use.

Environmental aspects have been considered right from the product creation process. To make recycling easier, all the plastic parts have been marked to show what they are made of.

178

Mia Seeger Stiftung   **Mia Seeger Foundation**

Mia Seeger   **Preis 2008**
Prize 2008

Jury
Judges panel

Prof. Karin Kirsch
Stuttgart

Heike Schnabel
Schnabel, Schneider Industrial Design
Schorndorf

Juliane Grützner
Redaktion design report
Leinfelden-Echterdingen

Margarete Wies
Mercedes-Benz Design, Daimler AG
Sindelfingen

Michael Daubner
Geschäftsführer Burkhardt Leitner constructiv GmbH
Stuttgart

Tom Schönherr
Phoenix Design
Stuttgart

Mia Seeger, 1927

Ausgezeichnet werden Diplomarbeiten aus den Jahren 2006 bis 2008. Bei der Bewertung der eingereichten Arbeiten ist neben den üblichen Designkriterien der soziale Nutzen entscheidend.

Undergraduate dissertations from 2006 to 2008 are eligible for entry. Apart from the usual design criteria, the decisive benchmark when assessing the studies submitted is their social utility.

Jährlicher Wettbewerb der Mia Seeger Stiftung für junge Designerinnen und Designer – Absolventen der Studiengänge Industriedesign / Produktgestaltung, Innenarchitektur / Möbeldesign, Architektur, Investitionsgüter- oder Transportation Design an deutschen Hochschulen

Preissumme 10.000 Euro

Annual competition organized by the Mia Seeger Stiftung for young designers – graduates from courses in Industrial Design/Product Design, Interior Design/Furniture Design, Architecture, Capital Goods Design or Transportation Design at German institutes of higher education

Total prize money: 10,000 euros

SRD   Sea Rescue Device

Mia Seeger Preis 2008
1. Preis

Mia Seeger Prize 2008
1st Prize

SRD   Sea Rescue Device

Entwerfer / Developer
Christian Westarp

Hochschule / University
Hochschule Darmstadt

Betreuung / Support
Prof. Tom Philipps

Christian Westarp
Gailbacher Straße 39
D-63743 Aschaffenburg
c.wes@wes-id.com

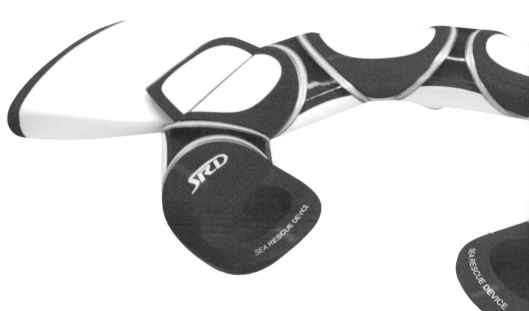

Jury
Den über Bord Gegangenen zu finden
und im Auge zu behalten, ist als Voraus-
setzung einer raschen Rettung erkannt
und hier als primäre Aufgabe formuliert.
Dafür wird eine technisch und formal
anspruchsvolle Lösung entwickelt. Span-
nungsvoll verbinden sich darin der Sinn
für die raue Realität der See, der Blick für
technologische Potenziale und die Lust
am morphologischen Spiel.

Judges panel
The design is based on the realization that
finding the man overboard and keeping
an eye on him is the condition for speedy
rescue. It focuses on achieving this condition, and comes up with a technically
and formally sophisticated solution. It
is an exciting combination of a sense of
the tough reality of sea conditions, of
a view for technological potential, and of
a pleasure in morphological games.

Mann über Bord? – Dann gibt sein Sender Alarm.
SRD löst sich automatisch vom Rumpf des
Schiffes und bewegt sich langestreckt und dü-
sengetrieben zum Opfer hin.

Sender, Radar und GPS besorgen die Steuerung.
Sensibel durch Sensoren, schlingt es sich um
den Verunglückten, indem es die Segmente ge-
genseitig verdreht.

Vor Ort aufgeblasene Luftkissen heben dessen
Kopf über Wasser. So gehalten und auch auf-
fällig markiert, steigen die Chancen für eine Ber-
gung auch bei rauem Wasser und auf hoher See.

Man overboard? His transmitter raises the alarm.
SRD releases itself automatically from the ship's
hull and, by means of jet propulsion, heads for the
victim.

At this stage, the SRD is extended to its full length.
The transmitter, radar and GPS ensure that it
takes the right direction. With the aid of sensors it
then curls itself around the victim, turning its
segments against each other.

Airbags inflated on the spot lift the victim's head
out of the water. Supported in this way, and clearly
marked, the victim has a better chance of being
rescued, even in heavy seas or on the open sea.

182

Mia Seeger Preis 2008
2. Preis

Mia Seeger Prize 2008
2nd Prize

rescue.kit **Interaktiver Rettungsassistent**
Interactive life-saver assistant

Entwerfer / Developer
Anika-Verena Letsche

Hochschule / University
Hochschule für Gestaltung Schwäbisch Gmünd

Betreuung / Support
Prof. Gerhard Reichert
Prof. Frank Zebner

Anika-Verena Letsche
Theodor-Heuss-Straße 32
D-89250 Senden
av.letsche@gmail.com

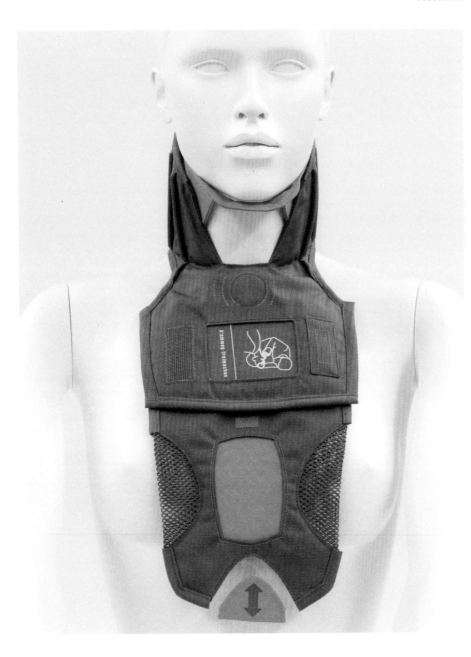

Jury
Wer Zeuge eines Notfalls mit Herzstill-
stand wird, hat in der Regel Angst, dass
er aus Unkenntnis oder Schreck lebens-
rettende Maßnahmen nicht oder nicht
richtig ausführen kann. Diesem Hin-
dernis abzuhelfen, ist »rescue.kit« entwickelt, vor allem für Laienersthelfer.
Dass die Rettungshilfe die zugleich physische wie kommunikative Mittlerrolle
zwischen Helfer und Hilfsbedürftigem
übernehmen kann, ist ihrer textilen Ausführung zu danken.

Judges panel
Anyone who is witness to an emergency
involving cardiac arrest is generally afraid
that they will not, or not properly, be
able to carry out life-saving measures because of inability or fright. »rescue.kit«
has been developed to help overcome
this obstacle, especially when first aid is
being given by unqualified helpers. Due
to its textile design, the life-saver aid acts
as both a physical and a communicative
intermediary between the helper and the
patient.

Ratloser Retter? – Nicht, wenn die Rettungshilfe
ihn beim Helfen anleitet. Er legt den interaktiven
Rettungsassistenten dem Bewusstlosen um den
Hals, wo die Vitalfunktionen gemessen werden,
und auf die Brust.

Display und Lautsprecher geben sodann Anweisungen, wie, wo und wie lange Herzmassage bzw.
Beatmung zu leisten sind. Dehnungssensoren
kontrollieren die Qualität der Massage.

Die vereinfachte Version hiervon ist eine Rettungs-
weste, auf der Druckbereich und Anweisungen
in piktografischer Form aufgedruckt sind.

Lifesavers at a loss? Not if this life-saver aid gives
them instructions on how to proceed. Placing
the interactive life-saver assistant around the un-
conscious person's neck and on his chest allows
vital functions to be measured.

The display and loudspeaker then provide instructions as to how, where, and how long to give
cardiac massage or mouth-to-mouth resuscita-
tion. Expansion sensors monitor the quality of the
massage.

The simplified version of this product is a life vest
on which the pressure points and instructions
have been printed in pictographic form.

Home Chare   Ein Pflegestuhl
An invalid chair

Mia Seeger Preis 2008   Mia Seeger Prize 2008
3. Preis   3rd Prize

Home Chare   **Ein Pflegestuhl**
                  An invalid chair

Entwerfer / Developer
Christen Halter

Hochschule / University
Hochschule Darmstadt

Betreuung / Support
Prof. Tom Philipps

Christen Halter
Engelhardstraße 53
D-63450 Hanau
chris@c-h-design.de

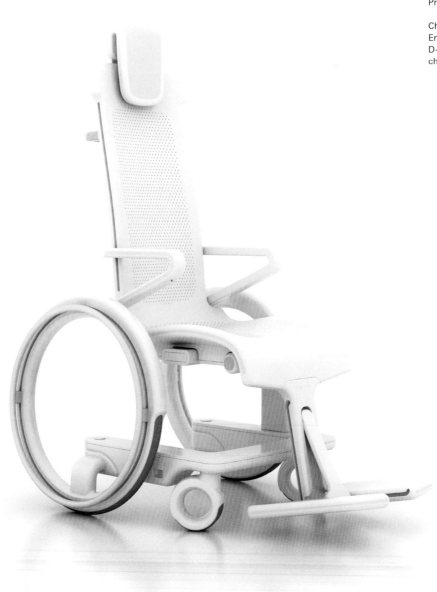

Jury
Klug ist die für den Sitz als durch elektroaktives Polymer bewirkt angenommene Kraftentfaltung mit der durch Transportmodule und Anbindungskomponenten bereitgestellten Variabilität kombiniert. So erst werden Hilfsgeräte wie der Lifter entbehrlich, gleichzeitig die Pfleger entlastet und die Patienten weniger gestresst.

Judges panel
What is clever about the chair is the way it combines the release of forces it assumes can be brought about by electroactive polymer and the variability provided by transport modules and transfer components. This obviates the need for any auxiliary apparatus such as invalid lifts, but also relieves the burden on the nurse and places the patient under less stress.

Wer hilft dem Helfer? – Ein Pflegestuhl, zusammengestellt aus den Baugruppen Sitz, Elektro-, Indoor- oder Rollstuhl-Modul, Kfz- und Treppenlift-Anbindung oder Dockingstation, erleichtert ihm gerade das anstrengende Umsetzen, Anheben oder Aufstellen der Pflegebedürftigen.

Der entscheidende Kunstgriff liegt darin, in den Schichtaufbau der Sitzfläche elektroaktive Polymerfolien so einzubauen, dass das Anlegen von Spannung an den gewünschten Stellen eine Wölbung hervorruft. Damit verschmelzen Antriebstechnik und Hülle; Scharniere und Drehachsen erübrigen sich.

Who helps the helper? An invalid chair comprising seat, electrical module, indoor module and wheelchair module, vehicle and stair-lift transfer or docking station makes it easier for the helper to move, lift or reposition the invalid.

The trick of the design is to insert electro-active polymer sheets into the layers making up the seat surface in such a way that a bulge is formed in the right places when an electrical current is applied. Surface and drive technology become one – there is no need for hinges or swivelling axles.

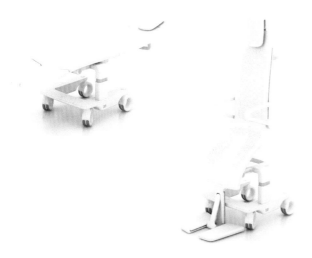

186

Mia Seeger Preis 2008   Mia Seeger Prize 2008
3. Preis   3rd Prize

känguru   **Tragesystem für Kleinkinder**
Carrying system for small children

Entwerfer / Developer
Oliver Klein

Hochschule / University
Kunsthochschule Berlin-Weißensee

Betreuung / Support
Prof. Helmut Staubach

Jury
Wer die umweltfreundlichsten Verkehrs-
mittel – Schuhwerk und Fahrrad – be-
vorzugt und ein Kleinkind mitnehmen
will, hat mit »känguru« eine gute, un-
komplizierte, formal ansprechende Lösung. Schutz und Sicherung des Kin-
des sind wohldurchdacht. So kann es
unbeschwert die elterliche Nähe und
ausreichend Aussicht genießen. Und weil
sorgfältig darauf geachtet ist, dass die
gesamte Konstruktion sehr leicht bleibt,
tragen die Eltern nicht gar so schwer.

Judges panel
Anyone who wants to use the most environmentally friendly form of travel –
walking boots or the bicycle – and wants
to take a small child with them will find
that känguru offers a good, uncomplicated, formally appealing solution. The
protection and safety of the child have
been given plenty of consideration. Without any inconvenience, it can remain
close to its parent and enjoy an unrestrict-
ed view. And because careful consideration has been given to keeping the entire structure very light, the burden is
not so heavy for the parents.

Wenn Mutter oder Vater radeln oder flanieren,
dann braucht der halb- bis zweijährige Nachwuchs nicht daheim zu versauern. Eine Sitzwie-
ge mit Sicherungsgurten und Kopfstütze nimmt
ihn auf, birgt ihn am elterlichen Rücken oder po-
sitioniert ihn recht hochsitzend über dem Ge-
päckträger des Fahrrads.

Das Gestell spielt dabei die tragende Rolle, und
wenn die Erwachsenen vom Gehen zum Fahren
wechseln oder umgekehrt, bleibt dem Kind er-
spart, umgesetzt zu werden.

Für das Tragegestell ist nach dem Vorbild des
Röhrenknochens eines Albatros eine Hohlstruk-
tur vorgesehen, die im rapid-manufacturing-Ver-
fahren herzustellen wäre.

If mum or dad want to go for a bike ride or a walk,
there is no need for their six-month to two-year
old child to be left at home. The child can sit in this
cradle seat, equipped with safety belts and a
head rest, which can be carried on the parent's
back or on the bicycle luggage rack.

The key function here is played by the frame. If
the adults move from walking to riding, or vice
versa, the child does not have to be moved from
its seat.

Based on the hollow bones of the albatross, the
frame is designed as a tubular structure that
could be produced using a rapid manufacturing
process.

188

IUVO Produktprogramm für die MS-Basisbehandlung
Product range for basic treatment of MS

Entwerfer / Developer
Simone Winkler

Hochschule / University
Fachhochschule Coburg

Betreuung / Support
Prof. Gerhard Kampe

Simone Winkler
Carl-Schüller-Straße 46
D-95444 Bayreuth
simone_winkler@freenet.de

Jury
Der Komplex der therapeutisch erforderlichen, tagtäglichen Handgriffe und
Besorgungen ist mit dem Komplex der
bevorstehenden e-Health-Informations-
strukturen in Einklang gebracht. Die
Bedürfnisse des Kranken, seine Ängste
und alltäglichen Nöte, sind detailliert
bedacht, aber auch sein Wunsch, so weit
wie möglich mobil, unabhängig und
selbstständig zu bleiben. Diesem An-
spruch wird diese intelligente, unpräten-
tiöse Lösung gerecht.

Judges panel
Two areas have been combined harmo-
niously here – the complex of therapeu-
tically necessary, everyday actions and
chores, and the complex of imminent
e-health information structures. Patients'
needs, fears and everyday problems
have been given detailed attention, as well
as their desire to remain as mobile, independent and self-sufficient as possible.
This intelligent, unpretentious solution
does justice to all these considerations.

Wenn MS-Kranke reisen, dann wäre es gut, sie
hätten alle Utensilien für die Selbstinjektion dabei, wären bei Bedarf mit behandelnden Ärzten,
Apotheke oder Krankenkasse verbunden und
hätten auch sonst allerlei kommunikative Hilfestel-
lung. Das nun leisten Injektionsgerät und Basis-
station im Verein mit einem Behältersystem, das
beide Geräte, die Fertigspritzen, andere Medika-
mente, Tupfer und Pflaster aufnimmt und auch für
Kühlung sorgt. Die Stapelhöhe richtet sich nach
der Dauer der Reise. Selbstverständlich funktioniert alles genau so gut von zuhause aus.

When MS sufferers travel, it would be good if
they could have all the implements they need for
self-injection with them, if they could contact
their attending physician, pharmacist or health
insurer if necessary, and if they had other communicative aids at their fingertips. This need is
now met by this injection appliance and base
station in combination with a container system
that offers room for the two appliances, the disposable syringes, other drugs, swabs and plasters,
as well as keeping everything cool. The height
of the stack depends on the duration of the jour-
ney. And of course, the whole thing works just
as well at home.

Skylino Kinderrückhaltesystem im Flugzeug
Child restraint system for aeroplanes

Mia Seeger Preis 2008
Anerkennung

Mia Seeger Prize 2008
Highly commended

Skylino **Kinderrückhaltesystem im Flugzeug**
Child restraint system for aeroplanes

Entwerfer / Developer
Karsten Willmann

Hochschule / University
Hochschule für Technik und Wirtschaft
Dresden (FH)

Betreuung / Support
Prof. Holger Jahn
Prof. Peter Laabs

Karsten Willmann
Bismarckstraße 10
D-01257 Dresden
k.willmann@creative-brain.com

Jury
»Skylino« vermittelt Sicherheit, ohne massiv zu wirken. Treffsicher und mit Sinn für die Realität ist es in die vorhandenen Strukturen des Luftverkehrs eingefügt und schließt eine empfindliche Sicherheitslücke, die Gesetzgeber wie Fluggesellschaften bisher beschämend weit offen gelassen haben.

Judges panel
»Skylino« conveys a sense of security without appearing too unwieldy. With an eye for the right solution and a sense of what is realistic, it fits into existing aviation structures and closes a grave safety gap that has so far been left disgracefully open by legislators and airlines.

Darf ein Baby fliegen? – Im Flugzeug schon, im Fahrgastraum nicht. Also wird es festgehalten. Am Check-in erhalten Eltern mit Kleinkind (2 Monate bis 2 Jahre) eine Trage, die sich von üblichen, ähnlichen in vier Punkten unterscheidet: Verbindungsschloss zwischen kindlichem und elterlichem Geschirr, das während unkritischer Flugphasen gelöst werden kann; ständige Turbulenzsicherung; Rückenstabilisator mit angeformter Kopfstütze, der im Ernstfall plötzliche Beschleunigungskräfte abfängt; spezielle Halterung, die das Kind wie in einer Hängematte ruhen lässt und dabei die Beine des Erwachsenen entlastet.

Should a baby be allowed to fly? In an aeroplane, yes, but not on a seat of its own. So it has to be held tight. When they check in, parents who are flying with small children (aged between two months and two years) are given a carrier belt that differs in four ways from other similar belts. First, there is the buckle connecting the child's and the parent's belts, which can be loosened during uncritical flight phases. Second, there is the permanent turbulence catch, which remains engaged for the entire flight. Third, there is the back support with a shaped head rest which cushions any acceleration forces that may suddenly occur in an emergency. Finally, there is the special clip that allows the child to rest as though it was in a hammock, and takes the weight off the adult's legs at the same time.

190   **Mia Seeger Preis 2008**   **Mia Seeger Prize 2008**
      Anerkennung   **Highly commended**

Ninos AS & GL   **Produkte für Diabetiker**
Products for diabetics

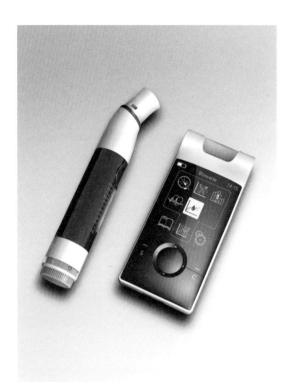

Entwerfer / Developer
Sascha Morawetz

Hochschule / University
Muthesius Kunsthochschule Kiel

Betreuung / Support
Prof. Ulrich Hirsch

Sascha Morawetz
Lastropsweg 37
D-20255 Kiel
saschamorawetz@gmx.de

Jury
Die vornehm elegante Gestaltung leitet
an zu diskreter und gewissenhafter Anwendung. Mehr aber zählt der Umstand,
dass beide Geräte der Therapie doch
wesentliche Unannehmlichkeiten nehmen. Dabei kommen Konzeption und
Entwurf ohne hypothetische Annahmen
hinsichtlich verfügbarer Technologien
aus.

Judges panel
The refined, elegant design encourages
discreet, conscientious use. More im-
portantly, the two appliances make treatment far less unpleasant. No hypotheti-
cal assumptions about the availability of
technologies were necessary for either
the concept or the design.

Nur ein Pieks? – Froh, dass es auch ohne geht,
ist, wer als Diabetiker häufig den Blutzucker
messen muss und regelmäßig Insulin, insbesondere kurz wirkendes zu den Mahlzeiten, benötigt. »Ninos GL« misst den Blutzucker, indem es
den Finger durchleuchtet und aus der Streu-
ung des Infrarotlichts den Glukoseanteil im Blut
errechnet. Zusätzlich erinnert es an die Messungen, dokumentiert sie für den Arzt, erstellt
Statistiken und speichert Notizen des Patienten.
»Ninos AS« ist ein Inhalator. Das Insulin ist der
Sprühflüssigkeit beigemengt und wird über die
Atemwege aufgenommen.

Just a prick? Any diabetic who frequently has
to measure their blood-sugar level and regularly
needs insulin, especially fast-acting insulin at
meal times, will be glad to do without just another
prick. »Ninos GL« measures blood sugar by
screening the patient's finger and using the scat-
ter of the infrared light to calculate the level of
glucose in the blood. In addition, it reminds patients to measure their blood sugar, documents
the results for the physician, prepares statistics
and saves patients' notes. »Ninos GL« is an in-
haler. The insulin is mixed into the spray liquid and
is absorbed in the respiratory tract.

Dentassist   Mobile Dentaleinheit
Mobile dental unit

Mia Seeger Preis 2008
Anerkennung

Mia Seeger Prize 2008
Highly commended

Dentassist   **Mobile Dentaleinheit**
Mobile dental unit

Entwerfer / Developer
Peer Hülsenbeck

Hochschule / University
Muthesius Kunsthochschule Kiel

Betreuung / Support
Prof. Ulrich Hirsch

Peer Hülsenbeck
Muhliusstraße 41
D-24103 Kiel
peerpost@gmx.net

Jury
Kostenträchtige und körperlich-seelisch belastende Transporte des Patienten zum Zahnarzt werden vermieden. In dieser Hinsicht ist ein wesentliches Problem erkannt und formal souverän gelöst. Die Zahnbehandlung kann jetzt für beide Beteiligten an dem ihnen vertrauten Platz stattfinden: für den Arzt »in seiner Praxis«, für den Patienten in seinem Lehnstuhl oder Bett.

Judges panel
There is no longer any need to transport patients to the dentist, which is both costly and physically and mentally distressing. In this respect, a pressing problem has been recognized, and solved in a formally masterful way. For both parties, dental treatment can now be performed in familiar surroundings: the dentist in his »surgery« and the patient in his armchair or bed.

Wenn der Zahnarzt kommt, z.B. im Altersheim, dann hat er seine Praxis im Rollcontainer dabei, nicht viel größer als ein Reisekoffer. Nachdem er die Deckplatte aufgeklappt, so eine gestufte Arbeits- bzw. Ablagefläche gewonnen, die mit Zuleitungen versehenen Instrumente in Stellung gebracht, den Wassertank befüllt und Strom angeschlossen hat, kann er in wenigen Minuten die Behandlung beginnen. Für die meisten altersüblichen Zahnerkrankungen ist er gerüstet.

If the dentist has to visit patients – for example, in an old people's home – then he can take his surgery with him in this trolley, which is not much bigger than a suitcase. Once he has opened the lid, and in doing so created a work surface, he then positions his instruments with their leads and tubes, fills the water tank and attaches the unit to the mains. This takes just a few minutes, and then treatment can begin. He is ready to treat most geriatric dental conditions.

Mia Seeger Stiftung
Foundation

Mia Seeger   **Stiftung**
Foundation

Mia Seeger Stiftung
c/o Design Center Stuttgart
im Haus der Wirtschaft
Willi-Bleicher-Straße 19
D-70174 Stuttgart
T +49 7 11 1 23 26 84 oder 26 86
F +49 7 11 1 23 27 71
E-mail tiziana.zamponi@rps.bwl.de
oder wolfgang.berger@rps.bwl.de

Ausführliche Informationen zur
Stiftung über Internet
www.mia-seeger.de oder bei der
Geschäftsstelle.

For more details about the Foundation, the Prize or the Scholarship,
visit www.mia-seeger.de or
contact the Foundation office,
Stuttgart

Impressum
Herausgeber: Mia Seeger Stiftung
Redaktion: Wolfgang Berger
Grafikdesign: Stapelberg & Fritz
Ausstellungsgestaltung: design hoch drei
Fotos: Preisträger und Ausgezeichnete

Publishing details
Published by: Mia Seeger Stiftung
Editor: Wolfgang Berger
Graphic design: Stapelberg & Fritz
Exhibition design: design hoch drei
Photographs: prize-winners and
commended entrants

Mia Seeger war die »Grande Dame« des Design.
Vor dem Zweiten Weltkrieg wirkte sie an großen
Ausstellungsprojekten des Deutschen Werk-
bundes mit, 1927 z.B. an der Weißenhofsiedlung
in Stuttgart. Nach dem Krieg führte sie als Prä-
sidialmitglied zwölf Jahre lang den Rat für Formgebung in Darmstadt. 1986 rief sie die nach ihr
benannte Stiftung ins Leben, deren Zweck die
Förderung der Bildung im Bereich Gestaltung
ist. Namhafte Sponsoren aus der Wirtschaft haben sich ihren Zielen angeschlossen. Mit der
Absicht, besonders den Nachwuchs im Design zu
fördern und ihn dabei zur Auseinandersetzung
mit sozialen Fragen herauszufordern, schreibt die
Stiftung jährlich den Mia Seeger Preis bundes-
weit aus, zusätzlich den Mia Seeger Förderpreis
zur Unterstützung von Projekten.

Mia Seeger was the »grand old lady« of design.
Before the Second World War, she was involved
in major exhibition projects of the Deutscher
Werkbund, such as the Weissenhof complex in
Stuttgart in 1927. After the war, she sat for twelve
years on the managing committee of the Rat
für Formgebung in Darmstadt. In 1986, she established the foundation that bears her name,
whose purpose is the comprehensive promotion
of education in design. Prominent sponsors from
the business world have lent their support to her
aims. With the aim of promoting young designers in particular, and of providing them with the
additional challenge of coming to terms with
social problems, the Foundation invites entrants
from all over Germany to compete for the annual Mia Seeger Award. There is also a Mia Seeger
Scholarship to support projects.

Adressen
Addresses

**Hersteller,
Designer, Vertriebe**

**Manufacturers,
designers, distributors**

A

AEG Design-Team
Muggenhoferstraße 135
D-90429 Nürnberg
T +49 1 71 3 06 14 95
hans.strohmeier@electrolux.de
www.aeg-electrolux.de

Seite / Page 104

Ulrich Alber GmbH
Vor dem Weißen Stein 21
D-74361 Albstadt
T +49 74 32 2 00 61 84
F +49 74 32 2 00 61 89
m.brunner@alber.de
www.alber.de

Seite / Page 80

Art Aqua GmbH & Co.
Prinz-Eugen-Straße 11
D-74321 Bietigheim-Bissingen
T +49 71 42 9 70 00
F +49 71 42 97 00 10
info@artaqua.de
www.artaqua.de

Seite / Page 46

**Ätztechnik Herz
GmbH & Co.**
Industriegebiet Kilbigswasen
D-78736 Epfendorf
T +49 74 04 9 21 40
F +49 74 04 92 14 30
info@aetztechnik-herz.de
www.aetztechnik-herz.de

Seite / Page 42

B

Design Ballendat
Martin Ballendat
Maximilianstraße 15
D-84359 Simbach
T +49 85 71 60 56 60
F +49 85 71 60 56 66
ballendat@ballendat.de
www.ballendat.de

Seite / Page 144

Bene Stuttgart
Breitwiesenstraße 19
D-70565 Stuttgart
T +49 7 11 3 41 81 80
F +49 7 11 34 18 18 99

Seite / Page 146

B/F Industrial Design
Christoph Böhler
Johannisstraße 3
D-90419 Nürnberg
T +49 9 11 9 33 69 70
F +49 9 11 93 36 97 50
welcome@bf-design.de
www.bf-design.de

Seite / Page 176

bgp-design
Knut Braake, Stefan Grobe
Lindenstraße 10
D-70563 Stuttgart
T +49 7 11 22 06 28 90
F +49 7 11 2 20 62 89 99
info@bgp-design.com
www.bgp-design.com

Seite / Page 26, 28

**Robert Bosch
Hausgeräte GmbH**
Carl-Wery-Straße 34
D-81739 München
T +49 89 45 90 02
F +49 89 45 90 23 47
www.bosch-hausgeraete.com

Seite / Page 102, 106

Werksdesign / In-house design
Ralph Staud,
Thomas Tischer

Seite / Page 106

Werksdesign / In-house design
Robert Sachon,
Alexander Marsch

Seite / Page 102

Brill Gloria
Haus- und Gartengeräte GmbH
Vertriebs- und Marketingzentrale
Edisonallee 3
D-89231 Neu-Ulm
T +49 7 31 1 40 60 44
F +49 7 31 1 40 60 55
a.werner@brillgloriagarten.com
www.brill.de
www.gloriagarten.de

Seite / Page 174

Brill Gloria
Haus- und Gartengeräte GmbH
Därmannsbusch 7
D-58456 Witten
T +49 23 02 7 00 45
F +49 23 02 7 00 46
a.werner@brillgloriagarten.com
www.brill.de
www.gloriagarten.de

Seite / Page 174

Brodbeck Design
Schillerstraße 40 C
D-80336 München
T +49 89 51 26 65 80
F +49 89 51 26 65 83
info@brodbeckdesign.de
www.brodbeckdesign.de

Seite / Page 148

Brühl
Brühl & Sippold GmbH
Alter Bad Stebener Weg 1
D-95138 Bad Steben-Carlsgrün
T +49 92 88 95 50
F +49 92 88 9 55 99
info@bruehl.com
www.bruehl.com

Seite / Page 130

Robert Bürkle GmbH
Stuttgarter Straße 123
D-72250 Freudenstadt
T +49 74 41 5 80
F +49 74 41 5 84 03
j.bender@buerkle-gmbh.de
www.buerkle-gmbh.de

Seite / Page 36

C

Constantine Furniture
Stang Schreinerei
Übrighäuserstraße 7
D-74547 Kupfer
T +49 79 44 95 00 88
F +49 79 44 95 00 89
www.constantine-furniture.com

Seite / Page 136

D

Dauphin
HumanDesign® Group GmbH & Co. KG
Espanstraße 36
D-91238 Offenhausen
T +49 91 58 1 77 00
F +49 91 58 1 77 01
info@dauphin-group.com
www.dauphin-group.com

Seite / Page 144

Design 3
Scharsteinwegsbrücke 2
D-20459 Hamburg
T +49 40 37 87 93 00
F +49 40 37 87 93 09
info@design3.de
www.design3.de

Seite / Page 158

Design Tech
Jürgen R. Schmid
Zeppelinstraße 53
D-72119 Ammerbuch
T +49 70 73 9 18 90
F +49 70 73 91 89 17
info@designtechschmid.de
www.designtechschmid.de

Seite / Page 36

B.T. Dibbern GmbH & Co. KG
Heinrich-Hertz-Straße 1
D-22941 Bargteheide
T +49 45 32 28 51 34
F +49 45 32 28 51 50
info@dibbern.de
www.dibbern.de

Seite / Page 120

Werksdesign / In-house design
Dibbern Design Studio

Seite / Page 120

Rolf Disch
SolarArchitektur
Merzhauser Straße 177
D-79100 Freiburg
T +49 7 61 45 94 40
F +49 7 61 45 94 44 44
info@rolfdisch.de
www.rolfdisch.de
www.plusenergiehaus.de

Seite / Page 48

DNS-Designteam
Kai-Uwe Neth + Ralph Schäflein
Erkelenzdamm 59 / Portal 2a
D-10999 Berlin
T +49 30 78 71 33 88
F +49 30 78 71 33 89
berlin@dns-design.de
www.dns-design.de

Seite / Page 168

E

Einmaleins
Büro für Gestaltung
Im Weitblick 1
D-88483 Burgrieden
T +49 73 92 96 96 11
F +49 73 92 96 96 22
m.weidt@einmaleins.net
www.einmaleins.net

Seite / Page 80

Eisele Kuberg Design
Frank Eisele
Oderstraße 1
D-89231 Neu-Ulm
T +49 7 31 9 80 75 55
F +49 7 31 9 80 75 56
info@eiselekubergdesign.de
www.eiselekubergdesign.de

Seite / Page 102

Eisfink
Max Maier GmbH & Co. KG
Rheinlandstraße 10
D-71636 Ludwigsburg
T +49 71 41 47 91 45
F +49 71 41 47 92 00
info@eisfink.de
www.eisfink.de

Seite / Page 96

Electrolux
Major Appliances Europe
Belgicastraat 17
B-1830 Zaventem
www.aeg-electrolux.de

Seite / Page 104

Electrolux Vertriebs GmbH
Muggenhoferstraße 135
D-90429 Nürnberg
www.aeg-electrolux.de

Seite / Page 104

Emeco
805 Elm Ave, Hanover
Hanover, Pennsylvania 17331
USA
T +1 40 19 35 70 88
alev@emeco.net
www.emeco.net

Seite / Page 126

EOOS Design GmbH
Zelinkagasse 2/6
A-1010 Wien
T +43 1 4 05 39 87
F +43 1 4 05 39 87 80
design@eoos.com
www.eoos.com

Seite / Page 128

Erlau AG
Erlau 16
D-73431 Aalen
T +49 73 61 5 04 17 42
F +49 73 61 5 04 12 88
erlau-ag@erlau.com
www.erlau.com

Seite / Page 50

Eva Denmark A/S
Måløv Teknikerby 18-20
DK-2760 Måløv
T +45 36 73 20 60
F +45 36 70 74 11
jeh@evadenmark.com
www.evasolo.com

Seite / Page 92, 112, 162, 172

F

Festo AG & Co. KG
Ruiter Straße 82
D-73734 Esslingen
T +49 7 11 34 70
www.festo.com

Seite / Page 30

Werksdesign / In-house design
Karoline Schmidt

Seite / Page 30

Forbo Flooring B.V.
Industrieweg 12
NL-1566 JP Assendelft
T +31 75 6 47 73 37
F +31 75 6 47 73 37
contact@forbo.com
www.forbo-flooring.com

Seite / Page 54

Werksdesign / In-house design
Josee de Pauw,
Tamar Gaylord

Seite / Page 54

Forbo Flooring GmbH
Steubenstraße 27
D-33100 Paderborn
T +49 5 25 11 80 30
F +49 5 25 11 80 33 12
www.forbo-flooring.com

Seite / Page 54

Foster + Partners Ltd.
Riverside
22 Hester Road
GB-London SW11 4AN
T +44 20 77 38 04 55
F +44 20 77 38 11 07
ssimpkin@fosterandpartners.com
www.fosterandpartners.com

Seite / Page 126

Naoto Fukasawa
S-17-20-4F Jingumae
Shibuya-KV Tokyo 150-0001
Japan
T +81 3 54 68 36 77
F +81 3 54 68 36 78
naoto@naotofukasawa.com
www.naotofukasawa.com

Seite / Page 156

G

Global-Mind-Network GmbH
Garde-du-Corps-Straße 5
D-34117 Kassel
T +49 5 61 81 04 80
F +49 5 61 8 10 48 28
office@global-mind.net
www.global-mind.net

Seite / Page 66

Möbelagentur Goeschen
Saidelsteig 78
D-91058 Erlangen
T +49 91 31 53 98 63
F +49 91 31 5 76 53
info@moebelagentur-goeschen.com
www.moebelagentur-goeschen.com

Seite / Page 126

H

H+W Bewässerungs GmbH
Steina 19
D-84364 Birnbach
T +49 85 63 35 93
F +49 85 63 9 16 61
bernhard.haering@
haering-gruenplan.de
www.haering-gruenplan.de

Seite / Page 46

Christen Halter
Engelhardstraße 53
D-63450 Hanau
T +49 1 77 3 13 83 01
chris@c-h-design.de

Seite / Page 184

Hansgrohe AG
Auestraße 5-9
D-77761 Schiltach
T +49 78 36 51 30 09
F +49 78 36 51 11 70
public.relations@hansgrohe.com
www.hansgrohe.com

Seite / Page 88, 90

**Hansgrohe
Deutschland Vertriebs GmbH**
Auestraße 5-9
D-77761 Schiltach
T +49 78 36 5 10
F +49 78 36 51 13 00
www.hansgrohe.com

Seite / Page 88, 90

Helios Ventilatoren GmbH + Co.
Lupfenstraße 8
D-78056 Villingen-Schwenningen
T +49 77 20 60 60
F +49 77 20 60 61 66
info@heliosventilatoren.de
www.heliosventilatoren.de

Seite / Page 68

Nannette Hopf
Bildstraße 3
D-70839 Gerlingen
T +49 71 56 2 64 44
F +49 71 56 71 14 79
nannette-hopf@filztex.de
www.filztex.de

Seite / Page 42

Peer Hülsenbeck
Muhliusstraße 41
D-24103 Kiel
T +49 1 79 3 99 59 84
peerpost@gmx.net

Seite / Page 191

Humanscale
11 East 26th Street, 8th Floor
New York, NY 10010
USA
T +1 2 12 7 25 47 49
F +1 2 12 7 25 75 45
info@humanscale.com
www.humanscale.com

Seite / Page 146

Humanscale Design Studio
Manuel Saez, Lachezar Tsvetanov,
Emilian Dan Cartis
147 West 26th Street, Suite 200
New York, NY 10001
USA
T +1 6 46 3 67 51 10
F +1 6 46 3 67 51 13
designstudio@humanscale.com
www.humanscaledesign.com

Seite / Page 146

I

**Ideenhaus
Kommunikationsagentur GmbH**
Findelgasse 10
D-90402 Nürnberg
T +49 9 11 9 33 57 34
F +49 9 11 39 60 66
florian.defren@ideenhaus.de
www.ideenhaus.de

Seite / Page 154

IKTD
Institut für Konstruktionstechnik und
Technisches Design
Universität Stuttgart
Thomas Maier
Pfaffenwaldring 9
D-70569 Stuttgart
T +49 7 11 68 56 60 60
F +49 7 11 68 56 62 19
thomas.maier@iktd.uni-stuttgart.de
www.iktd.uni-stuttgart.de

Seite / Page 32

Imago Design
Mitterstraßweg 19
D-82064 Straßbach
T +49 81 70 99 84 10
F +49 81 70 99 84 22
info@imago-design.de
www.imago-design.de

Seite / Page 68

Indoorlandscaping GmbH
Am Kiewelsberg 31
D-54295 Trier
T +49 1 71 4 80 48 04
F +49 1 71 1 34 80 48 04
look@indoorlandscaping.com
www.indoorlandscaping.com

Seite / Page 46

K

Alfred Kärcher GmbH & Co. KG
Alfred-Kärcher-Straße 28 - 40
D-71364 Winnenden
T +49 71 95 14 34 51
F +49 71 95 14 28 02
info@kaercher.de
www.kaercher.de

Seite / Page 38, 176

Alfred Kärcher Vertriebs-GmbH
Friedrich-List-Straße 4
D-71364 Winnenden
T +49 71 95 90 30
F +49 71 95 9 03 28 05
www.kaercher.de

Seite / Page 38, 176

Werksdesign / In-house design
Denis Dammköhler

Seite / Page 38

Werksdesign / In-house design
Michael Meyer

Seite / Page 176

Karl-Leibinger Medizintechnik
Kolbinger Straße 10
D-78570 Mühlheim
T +49 74 61 70 64 55
F +49 74 61 70 62 03
sales@KLSMartin.com
www.KLSMartin.com

Seite / Page 86

Oliver Klein
Ueckermünder Straße 5
D-10439 Berlin
T +49 1 63 8 67 85 92
oliver@lieblingsschuh.de

Seite / Page 186

Walter Knoll AG & Co. KG
Bahnhofstraße 25
D-71083 Herrenberg
T +49 70 32 20 80
F +49 70 32 20 83 90
info@walterknoll.de
www.walterknoll.de

Seite / Page 128

Kuball & Kempe
Alter Fischmarkt 11
D-20457 Hamburg
T +49 40 30 38 22 00
F +49 40 30 38 22 01

Seite / Page 170

L

C. Josef Lamy GmbH
Genzhöfer Weg 32
D-69123 Heidelberg
T +49 62 21 84 31 47
F +49 62 21 84 31 21
marco.achenbach@lamy.de
www.lamy.de

Seite / Page 156

Lemonfish® GmbH
Im Rank 10
D-73655 Plüderhausen
T +49 71 81 9 94 35 29
F +49 71 81 9 94 35 34
info@lemonfish.de
www.lemonfish.de

Seite / Page 166

Anika-Verena Letsche
Theodor-Heuss-Straße 32
D-89250 Senden
T +49 1 76 48 27 32 04
av.letsche@gmail.com

Seite / Page 182

Loewe Opta GmbH
Industriestraße 11
D-96317 Kronach
T +49 92 61 9 95 02
F +49 92 61 9 96 14
thorsten.kuerzinger@loewe.de
www.loewe.de

Seite / Page 158

**Loewe Opta GmbH
Vertrieb**
Industriestraße 11
D-96317 Kronach
T +49 92 61 9 96 07
F +49 92 61 9 92 46
www.loewe.de

Seite / Page 158

Glen Oliver Löw
Industrial Design
Loogeplatz 1
D-20249 Hamburg
T +49 40 27 80 82 09
mail@glenoliverloew.de
www.glenoliverloew.de

Seite / Page 140

M

Macharten
Nebeniusstraße 8
D-76137 Karlsruhe
T +49 7 21 3 54 08 32
F +49 7 21 3 54 08 33
info@macharten.com
www.macharten.com

Seite / Page 164

Werksdesign / In-house design
Monika Assem
monika.assem@macharten.com

Seite / Page 164

Christoffer Martens/erstererster
Gneisstraße 11
D-10437 Berlin
T +49 30 41 72 23 38
christoffer-martens@erstererster.de
www.christoffer-martens.de

Seite / Page 132

Maywerk Gmbh
Treppenstraße 17
D-42115 Wuppertal
T +49 2 02 4 46 98 00
F +49 2 02 4 46 98 01
info@maywerk.de
www.maywerk.de

Seite / Page 114

Werksdesign / In-house design
Hannes Mayer

Seite / Page 114

Melzer-Müller
Industrial Design
Wasenstraße 22
CH-8280 Kreuzlingen
T +41 71 6 88 42 34
F +41 71 6 88 42 35
melzermueller@bluewin.ch
www.melzermueller.ch

Seite / Page 62

Kati Meyer-Brühl
Ehrlich 9
D-95138 Bad Steben-Carlsgrün
www.bruehl.com

Seite / Page 130

Miele & Cie. KG
Carl-Miele-Straße 29
D-33332 Gütersloh
T +49 52 41 89 41 94
F +49 52 41 89 41 40
info@miele.de
www.miele.de

Seite / Page 40, 98, 100

Werksdesign / In-house design
Andreas Enslin

Seite / Page 40, 98, 100

Nils Holger Moormann GmbH
An der Festhalle 2
D-83229 Aschau im Chiemgau
T +49 80 52 9 04 50
F +49 80 52 90 45 45
info@moormann.de
www.moormann.de

Seite / Page 132, 134

Sascha Morawetz
Lastropsweg 37
D-20255 Kiel
T +49 1 76 20 38 40 66
saschamorawetz@gmx.de

Seite / Page 190

N

Nimbus Group GmbH
Sieglestraße 41
D-70469 Stuttgart
T +49 7 11 63 30 14 20
F +49 7 11 63 30 14 14
info@nimbus-group.com
www.nimbus-group.com

Seite / Page 72, 74

Werksdesign / In-house design
Dietrich Brennenstuhl

Seite / Page 72, 74

Nordwind
Energieanlagen GmbH
Lindenstraße 63
D-17033 Neubrandenburg
T +49 3 95 4 29 14 34
F +49 3 95 4 29 14 30
info@nordwind-energieanlagen.de
www.nordwind-energieanlagen.de

Seite / Page 58

O

Osram GmbH
Hellabrunner Straße 1
D-81543 München
T +49 89 6 21 30
F +49 89 62 13 20 20
r.wrenger@osram.de
www.osram.de
www.osram.de/evg-lms

Seite / Page 60

P

Pearl Creative GmbH
Tim Storti, Christian Rummel, Max Maier
Rheinlandstraße 10
D-71636 Ludwigsburg
T +49 71 41 4 88 74 90
F +49 71 41 4 88 74 99
info@pearlcreative.com
www.pearlcreative.com

Seite / Page 38, 96

Phoenix Design
Kölner Straße 16
D-70376 Stuttgart
T +49 7 11 9 55 97 60
F +49 7 11 55 93 92
info@phoenixdesign.de
www.phoenixdesign.de

Seite / Page 64, 88, 90

Plasmatreat GmbH
Bisamweg 10
D-33803 Steinhagen
T +49 52 02 9 96 00
F +49 52 02 99 60 34
mail@plasmatreat.de
www.plasmatreat.de

Seite / Page 28

Pure Position
Heinrichstraße 15
D-60327 Frankfurt
T +49 69 97 82 43 72
F +49 69 97 82 43 78
Info@pureposition.de
www.growingtable.de

Seite / Page 152

Werksdesign / In-house design
Olaf Schroeder
os@id-os.de
www.id-os.de

Seite / Page 152

Q

Quooker®
Peteri B.V.
Staalstraat 13
NL-2984 AJ Ridderkerk
T +31 1 80 42 04 88
F +31 1 80 42 88 09
info@quooker.nl
www.quooker.com

Seite / Page 122

Quooker® Deutschland GmbH
Marc Brinker
Kronprinzenstraße 138
D-40217 Düsseldorf
T +49 2 11 30 03 69 95
m.brinker@quooker.de
www.quooker.com

Seite / Page 122

R

RED
Research Engineering Design
Wilhelmstraße 5a
D-70182 Stuttgart
T +49 7 11 49 09 90 70
F +49 7 11 49 09 90 99
mail@teg.fhg.de
www.redproducts.de

Seite / Page 82

Rudolf Riester GmbH & Co. KG
Bruckstraße 31
D-72417 Jungingen
T +49 74 77 92 70 43
F +49 74 77 92 70 70
kleiner@riester.de
www.riester.de

Seite / Page 82

RTE
Akustik + Prüftechnik GmbH
Gewerbestraße 26
D-76327 Pfinztal/Karlsruhe
T +49 7 21 94 65 00
F +49 7 21 9 46 50 80
i.hertlin@rte.de
www.rte.de

Seite / Page 26

RUD Ketten
Rieger & Dietz GmbH & Co. KG
Friedensinsel
D-73432 Aalen-Unterkochen
T +49 73 61 5 04 17 42
F +49 73 61 5 04 12 88
sven.cravotta@rud.com
www.rud.com

Seite / Page 34

S

Schumann
Büro für industrielle Formentwicklung
Angelsachsenweg 72
D-48167 Münster
T +49 2 51 1 36 55 55
F +49 2 51 1 36 55 56
mail@schumanndesign.de
www.schumanndesign.de

Seite / Page 58

Siemens-Electrogeräte GmbH
Carl-Wery-Strasse 34
D-81739 München
T +49 89 45 90 09
F +49 89 45 90 23 47
www.siemens-hausgeraete.de

Seite / Page 108

Werksdesign / In-house design
Christoph Becke, Max Eicher

Seite / Page 108

Sioux GmbH
Finkenweg 2-4
D-74399 Walheim
T +49 71 43 37 12 42
F +49 71 43 80 37 12 42
mqueisser@sioux.de
www.sioux.de

Seite / Page 170

Werksdesign / In-house design
Reinhold Schulz
rschulz@sioux.de

Seite / Page 170

Specht Modulare Ofensysteme
GmbH & Co. KG
Bahnhofstraße 2
D-35116 Hatzfeld
T +49 64 52 92 98 80
F +49 64 52 9 29 88 20
info@xeoos.de
www.xeoos.de

Seite / Page 66

Stabilo International GmbH
Schwanweg 1
D-90562 Heroldsberg
T +49 9 11 5 67 13 74
F +49 9 11 5 67 13 11
wolfgang.harrer@stabilo.com
www.stabilo.com

Seite / Page 154

Steelcase Werndl AG
Georg-Aicher-Straße 7
D-83026 Rosenheim
T +49 80 31 40 50
F +49 80 31 40 51 00
info@steelcase-werndl.de
www.steelcase-werndl.de

Seite / Page 140, 142, 148

Sunways AG
Photovoltaic Technology
Macairestraße 3-5
D-78467 Konstanz
T +49 75 31 99 67 70
F +49 75 31 99 67 74 44
info@sunways.de
www.sunways.de

Seite / Page 62

T

Tools Design®
Henrik Holbæk & Claus Jensen
Rentemestervej 23 A
DK-2400 Kopenhagen NV
T +45 38 19 41 14
F +45 38 19 41 13
email@toolsdesign.dk
www.toolsdesign.dk

Seite / Page 92, 112, 162, 172

Trumpf Grüsch AG
Elektrowerkzeuge
Ausserfeld
CH-7214 Grüsch GR
T +41 81 307 61 61
F +41 81 307 64 16
info@ch.trumpf.com
www.trumpf-powertools.com

Seite / Page 32

**Trumpf Werkzeugmaschinen
GmbH & Co. KG**
Johann-Maus-Straße 2
D-71254 Ditzingen
T +49 71 56 30 30
F +49 71 56 30 33 09
info@trumpf.com
www.trumpf.com

Seite / Page 32

Tupperware Belgium N.V.
Wijngaardveld 17
B-9300 Aalst
T +32 53 72 72 11
F +32 53 72 72 10
yvetteverleysen@tupperware.com
www.tupperware.com

Seite / Page 116

Werksdesign / In-house design
Vincent Jalet
vincentjalet@tupperware.com

Seite / Page 116

Tupperware Belgium N.V.
Jan-Hendrik de Groote,
Dimitri Backaert
Wijngaardveld 17
B-9300 Aalst
T +32 53 72 75 42
F +32 53 72 75 40
jandegroote@tupperware.com
www.tupperware.com

Seite / Page 118

Tupperware Deutschland GmbH
Praunheimer Landstraße 70
D-60488 Frankfurt a. M.
T +49 69 76 80 20
F +49 69 76 80 22 99
www.tupperware.com

Seite / Page 116, 118

Tupperware France S.A.
Route de Monts
F-37300 Joué-lès-Tours
T +33 2 47 68 10 00
F +33 2 47 68 10 01
www.tupperware.com

Seite / Page 118

V

Viessmann Werke GmbH & Co. KG
D-35107 Allendorf
T +49 64 52 70 22 98
F +49 64 52 70 52 98
wee@viessmann.com
www.viessmann.com

Seite / Page 64

W

Weinberg & Ruf
Produktgestaltung
Martinstraße 5
D-70794 Filderstadt
T +49 7 11 7 08 50 10
F +49 7 11 7 08 50 18
info@weinberg-ruf.de
www.weinberg-ruf.de

Seite / Page 86, 174

Werzalit GmbH + Co. KG
Gronauer Straße 70
D-71720 Oberstenfeld
T +49 70 62 5 00
F +49 70 62 5 02 08
info@werzalit.de
www.werzalit.de

Seite / Page 52

Werksdesign / In-house design
Jörg Golombek

Seite / Page 52

Christina Weskott
Finger- und Handorthesen
Horbeller Straße 43
D-50858 Köln
T +49 22 34 27 10 60
F +49 22 34 27 10 69
atelier@christina-weskott.de
www.rheuma-ringe.de

Seite / Page 84

Christian Westarp
Gailbacher Straße 39
D-63743 Aschaffenburg
T +49 1 79 4 79 34 71
c.wes@wes-id.com

Seite / Page 180

Simon Wilkinson
C10 design & development bv
Zijlweg 76
NL-2013 DK Haarlem
T +31 23 5 51 36 00
F +31 23 5 42 19 50
info@C10.nl
www.C10.nl

Seite / Page 142

Karsten Willmann
Bismarckstraße 10
D-01257 Dresden
T +49 1 77 2 46 46 12 oder
T +49 3 51 2 07 54 99
k.willmann@creative-brain.com

Seite / Page 189

Simone Winkler
Carl-Schüller-Straße 46
D-95444 Bayreuth
T +49 1 75 7 13 43 22
simone_winkler@freenet.de

Seite / Page 188

Z

Züco Bürositzmöbel AG
Staatsstraße 77
CH-9445 Rebstein
T +41 71 7 75 87 87
F +41 71 7 75 87 97
mail@zueco.com
www.zueco.com

Seite / Page 144

Zweibrüder
Optoelectronics GmbH
Kronenstraße 5-7
D-42699 Solingen
T +49 2 12 5 94 80
F +49 2 12 5 94 82 00
info@zweibrueder.com
www.zweibrueder.com

Seite / Page 76

Werksdesign / In-house design
Stefan Feustel,
Harald Opolka

Seite / Page 76

Die fettgedruckten Seitenzahlen verweisen auf den Katalogteil, die mager gedruckten führen zum Adressenverzeichnis.

Page numbers in bold type refer to the catalogue section, while those in lightface type refer to the index of addresses.

204

Internationaler Designpreis Baden-Württemberg und Mia Seeger Preis 2008

Baden-Württemberg International Design Award and Mia Seeger Prize 2008

Impressum
Publishing details

Herausgeber / Editor
Design Center Stuttgart
Regierungspräsidium Stuttgart
Willi-Bleicher-Straße 19
D-70174 Stuttgart
T +49 7 11 1 23 26 84
design@rps.bwl.de
www.design-center.de

Text und Redaktion /
Text and editorial supervision
Andrea Scholtz M.A.
büro wortgewandt, Stuttgart

Übersetzung / Translation
Philip Mann, Marbach

Grafikdesign / Graphic design
stapelberg&fritz, Stuttgart
mit Kristina Böcker

Lithografie / Lithography
ctrl-s prepress GmbH, Stuttgart

Druck / Printing
Leibfarth & Schwarz GmbH & Co. KG
Dettingen/Erms

Produktion / Production
Meike Pätzold, Stuttgart

Papier / Paper
Juwel Offset, PEFC zertifiziert

Verlag und Vertrieb /
Publishing and distribution
avedition GmbH
Königsallee 57
D-71638 Ludwigsburg
T +49 71 41 1 47 73 91
kontakt@avedition.de
www.avedition.de

© 2008
avedition GmbH Ludwigsburg,
Design Center Stuttgart
und die Autoren / and the authors

Die Publikation erscheint
anlässlich der Ausstellung

»Focus Green – Internationaler
Designpreis Baden-Württemberg 2008
und Mia Seeger Preis 2008«

18. Oktober bis 30. November 2008

This catalogue is published to
accompany the exhibition

»Focus Green — Baden-Württemberg
International Design Award 2008
and Mia Seeger Prize 2008«

18 October to 30 November 2008

Veranstalter / Organizer
Design Center Stuttgart
Regierungspräsidium Stuttgart
Willi-Bleicher-Straße 19
D-70174 Stuttgart
T +49 7 11 1 23 26 84

Projektleitung / Project manager
Sabine Lenk

Organisation / Administration
Hildegard Hild
Michael Kern

Ausstellungsgestaltung /
Exhibition design
design hoch drei, Stuttgart

Inszenierung Preisverleihung /
Production of award-giving ceremony
pulsmacher, Ludwigsburg

ISBN 978-3-89986-102-0

Printed in Germany